Property of.

Hw Hende

W9-DFY-353

THE TRUE FUNCTIONS OF THE
SUNDAY SCHOOL

This Book
presented to the

CHURCH
LIBRARY
by

Mrs. Betty Collings

Code 436-371, No. 1, Broadman Supplies, Nashville, Tenn. Printed in USA

The True Functions of the Sunday School

ARTHUR FLAKE

First Secretary of the Department of Sunday School Administration, Sunday School Board of the Southern Baptist Convention

NASHVILLE, TENNESSEE
THE SUNDAY SCHOOL BOARD
of the
SOUTHERN BAPTIST CONVENTION

Printed in the United States of America
3.5AL503

INTRODUCTION

The aim in producing this volume is threefold: first, to show the marvelous scope and reach of the work of the modern Sunday school; second, to show that each of the activities treated herein has an important place in the work of the Sunday school as now organized; third, to present clearly and positively practical methods for the accomplishment of each of these activities.

The desire and hope of the author is to crystallize in the thinking of pastors and churches a gripping knowledge of the fact that the Sunday school presents an unparalleled opportunity for the successful promotion of practically every phase of church activity as well as the utilization of every member of the church in useful service without detracting from the effectiveness of the Sunday school as a Bible teaching agency, or interfering, in the least degree, with the work of any other desirable and useful church agency.

It is not a new idea to regard the subjects discussed in this volume as logical parts or phases of Sunday school work. Quite a few churches are incorporating all of these activities in their programs with great effectiveness. However, in this study each of these phases is given a new emphasis, and is elevated to a place of major importance as a real and vital part of Sunday school endeavor.

Now, twenty or more years after this book was first offered, we are more than ever convinced of the truth of the principles which the author has set forth. Experience has multiplied the proofs of the soundness of his position.

DIRECTIONS FOR THE TEACHING AND STUDY OF THIS BOOK FOR CREDIT

I. *Directions for the Teacher*

1. Ten class periods of the forty-five minutes each, or the equivalent, are required for the completion of a book for credit.

2. The teacher is given, when requested, an award on the book taught.

3. The teacher shall give a written examination covering the subject matter in the textbook. The examination may take the form of assigned work to be done between the class sessions, in the class sessions, or as a final examination.

Exception: All who attend all of the class sessions; who read the book through by the close of the course; and who, in the judgment of the teacher, do the classwork satisfactorily may be exempted from taking the examination.

4. Application for Sunday school awards should be sent to the state Sunday school department, where forms may be secured on which to make application for awards. These forms should be made in duplication and both copies sent.

II. *Directions for the Student**

(*The student must be fifteen years of age or older to receive Sunday school credit.)

1. In Classwork
   (1) The student must attend at least six of the ten forty-five minute class periods to be entitled to take the the class examination.
   (2) The student must certify that the textbook has been read. (In rare cases where students may find it impracticable to read the book before the completion of the classwork, the teacher may accept a promise to read the book carefully within the next two weeks.)
   (3) The student must take a written examination, making a minimum grade of 70 per cent, or qualify according to *Exception* noted above.

2. In Individual Study by Correspondence
   Those who for any reason wish to study the book without the guidance of a teacher will use one of the following methods:
   (1) Write answers to the questions printed in the book, or
   (2) Write a development of the chapter outlines.
   In either case the student must read the book through.

   Students may find profit in studying the text together, but where awards are requested, individual papers are required.

   All written work done by such students on books for Sunday school credit should be sent to the state Sunday school secretary.

CONTENTS

[9]

THE SUNDAY SCHOOL TRAINING COURSE

The Sunday School Training Course prepared by the Sunday School Department of the Baptist Sunday School Board is one of the major means of promoting Sunday school work. Its influence is limited only by its use.

The six sections of the course include studies in Bible, doctrines, evangelism, Sunday school leadership and administration, teaching, age group studies, and special studies. The range of the course is broad, for the field of Sunday school work is broad and requires comprehensive and specific training. Sixteen books are required for the completion of each Diploma.

The study of the Training Course is not to be limited to the present Sunday school workers. Many churches need two or three times as many workers as are now enlisted. This need can be supplied by training additional workers now. Members of the Young People's and Adult classes and older Intermediates should be led to study these books for thereby will their service be assured. Parents will find help as they study what the Sunday school is trying to do.

Write to your state Sunday school secretary or to the Sunday School Department, Baptist Sunday School Board, Nashville 3, Tennessee, for a list of the books and other information.

SPECIAL NOTE TO INSTRUCTOR:

During your teaching of this book will you check with the Sunday school superintendent to see that an accurate record of training for the workers is kept. If not, please urge him to set up such a file with an associate superintendent of training in charge. File cards for this purpose will be supplied free of charge upon request. For further information write to the Sunday School Department, Baptist Sunday School Board, Nashville 3, Tennessee.

J. N. BARNETTE, *Secretary,*
Sunday School Department
Baptist Sunday School Board

CHAPTER I

THE SUNDAY SCHOOL DEFINED

Sunday schools in Baptist churches today "live and move and have their being" in the churches. They are in the churches, of the churches, and for the churches. This has not always been the case. In the beginning the Sunday schools were separate, independent bodies. The churches were slow to see the need for Sunday schools, and for a long time hesitated to give them a place among the regular activities. Even now, in some churches, the Sunday school is merely tolerated, and in only a few is it utilized to its fullest capacity.

These conditions exist because the leaders do not have a correct understanding of the true functions of the Sunday school. Many have sought to define its work in a sentence. The place and power of the Sunday school are too great and its activities too varied and wide in their scope for this to be done successfully.

I. SOME WRONG CONCEPTIONS OF THE SUNDAY SCHOOL

A limited view of the Sunday school has greatly hindered its work. Let us examine some of the more common misconceptions.

1. *Regarded as an Independent Body*

Even yet, hosts of good people think of the Sunday school as an organization sufficient in and of itself. There are still churches in which the Sunday school "cabinet" composed of the officers and teachers meets and elects the officers and teachers for the ensuing year. This procedure is entirely wrong. The Sunday school organization is not a deliberate body at all. It cannot make motions, enact laws for its own government, or elect its own officers and teachers. These functions belong to the church of which it is a part.

Sunday schools obsessed with the idea of their own independence, without exception, do poor work and often are sources of discord in the churches.

2. *Regarded as a Part of a Worldwide System of Religious Education.*

The interdenominational Sunday school leaders of the world hold to the idea that Sunday schools are a part of a worldwide system of religious education. A great majority of educators, both in secular and Christian schools, hold to this idea.

We wish to affirm that there is no organic relationship existing between Baptist Sunday schools and any agencies outside of the churches. Moreover, Sunday schools have no organic connection or relation to each other, not even Sunday schools in Baptist churches. Each is the agency of the church of which it is a part.

3. *Called the "Teaching Service" of the Church*

To define the Sunday school as a teaching service, in the narrow sense, is greatly to limit its power and usefulness. To be sure, teaching the Bible is the main business of the Sunday school. However, Bible truths have not been learned until they have been put into practice. Bible teaching in its fullest sense requires the Sunday school to function not only for an hour and a half on Sunday morning, but also as an effective church agency for carrying out the commands of Christ throughout each of the fifty-two weeks of the year.

4. *Called the "Child of the Church"*

The Sunday school is not a child at all. Such a desig-nation is a grave injustice. The Sunday school is a great Bible-teaching church agency. Its officers and teachers are church members. The pastor is the chief officer and the chief teacher. Every member of the church should be a member of the Sunday school. The officers of the Sunday school are accountable to the church, and they should make reports to the church as do the deacons, the trustees, the finance committee, or other church-elected officers.

5. *Looked Upon as an "Auxiliary" of the Church*

The term "auxiliary" carries the idea of a separate and independent organization, person, or institution associated by agreement as a helper in a cause. A Sun-day school is no more a church auxiliary than is one's hand or foot an auxiliary of his body. The Sunday school is a powerful means which a church may, and should, use for the promulgation of the gospel of Christ to the ends of the earth.

6. *Conducted as a "Mass Meeting"*

The "good old-fashioned Sunday school" which met as a mass meeting with the superintendent occupying the center of the stage has gone forever. Even in the most remote rural communities the Sunday schools of today are graded. Lessons are adapted to the needs of each age group; the officers and teachers are being trained, and modern buildings are rapidly supplanting the old one-room structures.

Today, we understand that the Sunday school exists for the purpose of meeting the spiritual needs of the pupils. The teacher is one who guides to the fountain of knowledge, and meeting pupil needs with the truths of the Bible is regarded as the main thing in the Sunday school session. The superintendent is chosen because of his ability as an executive rather than because he is a "good talker."

7. *Regarded as Primarily for Children*

In the beginning Sunday schools were thought of altogether in connection with children as pupils, and women (occasionally, perhaps a good man) as teachers. This conception of the Sunday school is difficult to eradicate from the minds of many people today.

There are still some pastors who feel that the Sunday school is not a part of their work. There are still some adults who do not see their need to get into a class on Sunday morning and study the Word of God. Even some Sunday school workers habitually use the feminine pronoun in speaking of the teachers and refer to the pupils as "children."

However, the last decades have revolutionized our conception. Today we seek to provide in the Sunday school for every member of every family. Men and women, as well as children, need to study the Word of God. In addition, a fully functioning Sunday school seeks to furnish a place of service for every resident church member.

8. *Regarded as Similar to the Secular School*

To regard the Sunday school as an educational institution to be organized, standardized, and operated like the secular school is most misleading.

The Sunday school is a real school, worthy of the highest type of teaching. But its purposes are distinctive, and the methods of organizing and operating secular schools do not apply.

For example, to grade Sunday school pupils on the scholarship basis, as is the case in the secular school, would disregard the spiritual needs common to each age group. It would discourage attendance, especially on the part of adults.

Likewise, to apply the same scholarship test to Sunday school workers as is applied to secular teachers would eliminate many of our most loyal, efficient, and powerful Sunday school officers and teachers.

The highest test of a Sunday school teacher's work is the number of pupils he is able to lead to Christ and develop in the Christian life. It is readily seen that such a test applied to the work of the secular school teacher is illogical and finds no place in our thinking in connection with his work.

In secular school there may be a time to give special honors and awards to those who excel their fellows. In the Sunday school all kinds of contests and rivalries are hurtful, and proficiency comes through self-effacement and a ceaseless desire to esteem others better than ourselves.

9. *Sunday School Work Not Considered "Church Work"*

This is perhaps the most common of all the mistaken ideas concerning the Sunday school. The Bible-teaching session Sunday morning is spoken of as the Sunday school, and the preaching service which immediately follows is spoken of as the "church service." These designations convey the idea that the preaching service is a church service, and that the Sunday school service is not a church service; that preaching is church work and that teaching the Bible in the Sunday school is not church work.

The Sunday school ministry of Bible teaching on Sunday morning is as much a church service as either the eleven o'clock preaching hour or the mid-week prayer meeting.

II. THE SUNDAY SCHOOL A CHURCH AGENCY FOR CARRYING OUT THE BAPTIST MISSION

There are those who, in the interest of church union, would question the need for our distinctive Baptist witness.

1. *Why Our Distinctive Mission Is Needed*

We believe that the world today needs the Baptist message as much as it ever did. Since Baptist churches are necessarily the custodians of this message, we believe that instead of reducing the number of churches by consolidation and otherwise, more Baptist churches should be organized until in time there is one within easy reach of every human being on the habitable part of the globe.

(1) *To proclaim the doctrine*

We believe that all the members of all Baptist churches should be thoroughly instructed in all the doctrines held by Baptists until each and every one of them is a thoroughly informed and highly useful Christian and able to give a reason for the faith that is in him.

Not only should the members of Baptist churches be given the Baptist message, but also, for Christ's sake and humanity's sake, the Baptist message should be proclaimed and the Baptist spirit promoted throughout the whole world.

We can greatly impair if not destroy the Baptist spirit by keeping silent on any of the fundamental teachings of the New Testament. The injunction in the Great Commission is: "teaching them to observe all things whatsoever I have commanded you." The apostle Paul said, "I have not shunned to declare unto you all the counsel of God."

Baptists have a divine commission to proclaim and to practice the whole truth. We dare not remain silent on any of the great doctrines of the New Testament.

In this connection, Dr. J. B. Gambrell said: "If we substitute platitudes and generalities and little sentimental nothings for the great doctrines of the Bible, the spirit will die. If one is to be a stalwart Christian of the New Testament order, he is to feel the solid rock of truth under his feet. . . .

"We can have unity only on the authority of Jesus Christ and his Word. . . . The world never went apart religiously until it quit the true center of unity. Now, the true Baptist spirit will stand loyally to the Word, which is the same as saying, [it will stand] loyally to the authority of Jesus. The true spirit will not even consider compromise which affects the integrity of the Word. I see nothing around the whole horizon so ominous as the letting down on the part of some Baptists in the matter of loyalty to the Word of God."

(2) *To practice the truth*

Southern Baptists have a great program for giving the whole gospel to the whole world. One of the best ways to promote the Baptist spirit is for our people everywhere to co-operate with our Baptist agencies for successfully carrying out this program.

Again we quote from Doctor Gambrell: "It is hard to think of a greater mistake than that which some of our brethren are making in that they contend ceaselessly for the doctrines and yet care little or nothing about the work. There no better way to dissipate the spirit than to stagnate the work. . . . The Baptist spirit is certain to die where the Baptists are doing nothing in a practical way for the world."

2. *The Sunday School Particularly Fitted to Promote the Baptist Spirit*

Baptist churches everywhere must use their Sunday schools as powerful agencies for promoting the Baptist spirit, both in doctrines and in practice.

The words of I. J. Van Ness written back in 1910 are still up-to-date: "One thing is certain—we have in the Sunday school of today the most perfect agency in the world for impressing ourselves as a denomination upon this and the coming generation. That the Sunday school ought to be used in some way for denominational upbuilding can hardly be a question. A denomination that does not care enough for its convictions to perpetuate them has no business being alive. It ought to get out of the way for those who do believe in something."

The Sunday school is particularly fitted to promote loyalty to all denominational agencies and to foster the whole mission of the church.

(1) *The people it reaches*

A Baptist church has in the Sunday school an organization of undreamed possibilities already set up through which to educate, train, and indoctrinate its people.

Here in the places of leadership are a large group of the most consecrated and intelligent members of the church, willing and ready to follow the leadership of the pastor in any and every worth-while way he may direct. They are among the ablest, the most powerful and most spiritually-minded workers in the church.

We also have in the Sunday school, meeting each week, the greatest number of people that the church can congregate at one time for any cause whatever. They come together each Sunday morning for study of the Bible. In this great throng we have not only the members of Baptist churches and the children whose parents are members, but also numbers of people who have no church affiliation.

The Sunday school is an ideal church agency for the promotion and cultivation of the Baptist spirit. What is needed is for our Baptist leaders, pastors, and Sunday school superintendents to enlarge their vision, increase the scope of their Sunday school perspective, and utilize effectively this powerful agency for the promotion of the Baptist spirit among the people.

(2) *The distinctive methods it uses*

The methods of Sunday school organization and administration now in vogue in Southern Baptist churches are peculiar to us. They are the outgrowth of our distinctive doctrines, and they serve to promote those doctrines.

These methods have grown out of actual experience. They have been stabilized and standardized. We have not changed at every suggestion from outside sources, no matter how important such suggestions may have appeared. We have given our standards and methods opportunity to demonstrate their merit. This they have invariably done to our satisfaction when given a fair chance.

We have not been against a change in methods if by changing we could improve our work, but we have not been quick to accept untried theories. Let us note some of the principles and practices advocated and promoted by Southern Baptists in their Sunday school work:

The principle of church control

The plans of grading and departmentization

The effective use of the weekly officers and teachers' meeting

The centrality of the Bible in the whole Sunday school program

The use of Baptist literature

The major emphasis on soul-winning

The specific training for officers and teachers

The promotion and use of a system of records which honors the Sunday school as a Bible teaching agency, and which stands for more than attendance and a collection

The intelligent use of Standards of Excellence as a means of guiding Sunday school workers in all parts of the Convention territory

The concern of Baptists for all people of all classes, as evidenced in sustained, systematic visitation

(3) *The Bible-centered teaching it offers*

All Southern Baptist lesson materials are designed to be both Bible-centered and pupil-centered. The Uniform Lesson Series is adapted to meet the needs of individuals from the Nursery through the Adult age groups in schools organized on the class basis.

The Graded Lesson Series is designed for schools having classes limited to a one-year age range in the departments below the Young People's. All the lessons are Bible-centered and closely graded to meet the needs of the pupils at each stage of their development.

No matter which lesson series is used in a school, the Bible is the textbook. Each pupil above eight years of age is encouraged to bring his Bible to the Sunday school and use it. The ministry of the teacher is to train his pupils in the use of the Bible through guided learning activities in the classroom and to stimulate and direct them in putting Bible truths into practice.

Certainly Baptists cannot afford to think even for one moment about substituting nature studies, biographical studies, or forums on social problems for Bible-centered lessons in any of the age groups. We must make the Bible central in all our Sunday school work. This we have done in the past and will continue to do until the end.

(4) *The opportunities it affords for informing the people*

One of the best ways of promoting the Baptist spirit is for our Sunday schools to follow the Calendar of Denominational Activities adopted by the Southern Baptist Convention. Through observing the special days, and through engaging in the activities suggested in this Calendar, our people can be educated in the work that Baptists are doing.

Only by a study of all of their missionary and benevolent enterprises and educational institutions can Baptists maintain the proper enthusiasm and spirit for their support. There can be no spirited, intelligent co-operation without this study. The Sunday school is an effective agency to acquaint Baptist people with the true condition of a needy world, the scope and plan of Southern Baptists to meet these needs, and the results which under divine favor have already been attained.

A Baptist church is a democracy and can function at its best only as all of the participants, both the leaders and those who follow, keep informed concerning the work. Baptists cannot thrive on ignorance. Baptist leaders must study constantly, and as constantly keep their people studying diligently all phases of Baptist work. This is the only way in which the work of all the organizations in a Baptist church can be correlated and made to harmonize.

Only informed Baptists can give the whole Baptist message proper expression. Just at this point the Baptist spirit is greatly impaired. There are literally hundreds of thousands of the rank and file of our church members not able to give proper expression to the Baptist message because they have not learned how to do this.

The task of Southern Baptist leaders is to inform this multitude of Baptist participants. This the Sunday school can do in a large measure if the leaders will avail themselves of the plans suggested in chapter 5.

The Baptist spirit is the spirit of conquest. There is not one good reason why Southern Baptists should sound a low note. The progress made in Sunday school work during the past twenty years reads like a romance.

God has yet greater achievements in store for us as churches everywhere come to see the true functions of the Sunday schools and to use them to the fullest extent in carrying out the divine commission.

III. THE SUNDAY SCHOOL RIGHTLY RELATED

If any Sunday school is to perform its greatest ministry, it must be rightly related to the program of the church. It must be directed by leaders who have a clear vision of its possibilities.

1. *The Officers and Teachers Elected by the Church*

The pastor is the chief officer in the Sunday school organization. The church should elect all the other officers and teachers in the Sunday school annually.

This is done by selecting a nominating committee, usually composed of the pastor and three other members of the church. This committee should nominate the superintendent at a regular business meeting of the church. The church may elect this nominee, or some one else, according to its own judgment. As soon as the superintendent is elected he should be added to the nominating committee for the selection and nomination of all the other officers and teachers.

Under no circumstances should the officers and teachers of the Sunday school elect their successors. This procedure develops a self-perpetuating organization and takes the control and direction of the Sunday school out of the hands of the church. Nor should Sunday school classes be allowed to nominate and elect teachers or supply teachers. This applies alike to all groups, including the adults.

2. *The Sunday School Supported by the Church*

The church should provide a meeting place for its Sunday school with sufficient rooms of the proper size. It should purchase all supplies, literature, and working equipment such as maps, charts, and so forth. The church should finance the entire educational and social program of its Sunday school. This should be mapped out in advance and approved by the church.

Every member of the church should belong to the Sunday school. A functioning Extension department will make this possible even for those who cannot attend. We must continue a loving ministry to lead all Southern Baptists to recognize their obligation to be enlisted members of the Sunday school.

3. *The Activities Defined and Governed by the Church*

Certainly the church must accept the responsibility for saying who shall serve as officers and teachers in its Sunday school. It should elect only men and women who will teach the Bible in its purity and uphold the doctrines of the church. The church must define the functions and control the operation of the Sunday school. This is done through two main Sunday school officials, the pastor and the superintendent, to whom the church intrusts the direction of the Sunday school. To these two men the operation of the Sunday school is committed, and they should be held accountable for its success or failure.

4. *A Monthly Report Made to the Church*

The superintendent should submit a monthly written report of the work of the Sunday school to the church. This may be commented upon by the pastor, the superintendent, and others. It should be adopted and spread upon the minutes of the church.

IV. THE TRUE FUNCTIONS OF THE SUNDAY SCHOOL UNDERSTOOD

What are the functions of the Sunday school as a church agency for carrying out Christ's commission to the church?

It must function as an agency to—

Teach all the fundamentals of the Bible to all the people according to their spiritual needs

Provide places of service and development for all the members of the church

Discover and reach the unenrolled and the unenlisted people

Provide training for all church members to develop them for larger service

Promote attendance at the preaching services and other meetings of the church

Magnify winning the lost to Christ as the heart of all the program

Instruct and enlist its members in a Spiritual program of church finance

Instruct and enlist its members in the mission program of the denomination

The remaining chapters of this book will discuss ways in which Sunday schools can fulfil their true functions.

There is an appendix carrying workbook suggestions for use in reviews. It contains a section based on each chapter. After the class discussion of chapter 1, turn to Section I of the appendix and use the instructions there as a guide to summarizing and applying the truths discussed.

CHAPTER II

THE SUNDAY SCHOOL FUNCTIONING AS A BIBLE TEACHING AGENCY

The simple, practical methods of Sunday school administration which are now being offered to Southern Baptists will cause Sunday schools to function as real Bible teaching agencies.

If adopted and used intelligently and vigorously by our churches, these methods will result in bringing into our Sunday schools a vast army of people who are waiting just outside the doors of Baptist churches in city, town, and rural communities alike. They will cause every one of these Sunday schools to be a powerful church agency for teaching the Word of God.

The Sunday school is organized and operated for the benefit of the pupils. The building in which the school meets should be erected and adjusted to meet the needs of the pupils. The lessons are made for them. The programs are arranged and given for their joy and edification. The Sunday school exists for the pupils and not for the officers and teachers as some seem to think.

Sometimes a superintendent is heard to speak of the Sunday school as "my school." He has it wrong. The officers and teachers belong to the Sunday school, and as servants of the church, working in the Sunday school, it is their privilege and duty so to give of their time, talents, and their all, that the Sunday school shall function effectually as a real Bible teaching school. Let us study some of the ways in which this may be done.

I. It Must Minister to Individuals

Each pupil must receive personal attention, though there are thousands in the Sunday school. Not one may be lost in the crowd. In the last analysis each Sunday school will have to stand the test at this point.

Let us see some of the things which the school must do to bring about the pupils' development and growth. All of these things are simple and easy under the guidance of good teachers and officers.

1. *Work for Regular and Prompt Attendance*

An irregular, tardy pupil is better than no pupil at all. But if he is to get the best things the Sunday school has in store for him, he must attend every session and attend on time. Irregularity and tardiness on the part of any member should be a challenge to the teacher and the class to lay themselves out in his behalf to help him correct these grievous faults.

A heart-to-heart talk will often help him to overcome his negative habits. Assigning him some phase of class activity such as going after other irregular members is an excellent way of helping him.

Finding fault and dropping names are both fatal. If a pupil attends once a month and always arrives during the lesson, it is better to have him then than not at all. There is always a hope for improvement. Sunday school officers and teachers should shoulder their responsibility at this point, and never grow negligent nor slacken their effort to have every member in his place on time at every session.

2. *Encourage Lesson Preparation*

This discussion is dealing with members of all grades and capacities. All, at least above Beginner ages, can be led to do a reasonable amount of lesson preparation, if teachers will study their interests, needs and abilities, and will offer suitable guidance for home study. No pupil of any age will ever learn much of the contents of the Bible if he does not study it for himself.

(1) *The pupils must exercise individual effort to learn*

Sunday school pupils are not receptacles into which teachers may pour Bible truths for thirty minutes on Sunday morning expecting them to be "full of the Scriptures," and as a result be good and useful all the week. It doesn't work that way. If individuals are ever to know much about the Word of God and grow in grace and spiritual power, they must engage in personal Bible study.

(2) *The teacher should expect pupils to study*

The teacher's part is all-important here. He should know his pupils individually, the traits and capacity of each, just what each one needs and just the methods to be employed in securing his co-operation in lesson study. If there is careful and prayerful planning of the lesson with each pupil in mind; if definite assignments for home study are made; if there is wise guidance in the lesson period so that each pupil will participate, then habits of good lesson preparation will be developed.

Making lesson study requirements of pupils will not drive them away. In fact, a real Bible-studying, Bible-teaching Sunday school will draw people of all classes and ages.

(3) *Small classes are essential*

Even at their best, large Sunday school classes of Adults and Young People with attractive orators as teachers will never function effectively in teaching the Bible. Until these large classes are replaced by small groups of not more than fifteen to twenty Young People and twenty-five to forty Adults, and until sharing learning activities replaces lecturing as the main method of teaching, there will never be the most effective Bible learning by the rank and file of members of the Young People's and Adult departments.

3. *Plan for Bringing and Using Bibles*

It is time to get down to business and stop quibbling over the important matter of bringing and using Bibles. We have a Bible school and the majority of the members are Christians. They say they love and believe the Bible. Yet we find classes of grown men and women apparently using every subterfuge possible to keep from bringing their Bibles to the Sunday school. We also find pastors, superintendents, and teachers seemingly giving them comfort by agreeing that they ought to be excused from bringing the Word of God to the house of God. This is a shameful situation and a change in attitude is needed immediately.

If officers and teachers will bring their Bibles to Sunday school, if they will encourage the members to bring theirs and use them in the assemblies and the lesson periods, soon the pupils from the Junior to the Adult age groups will respond.

The chief responsibility at this point rests upon the teacher. Certainly a pupil cannot use his Bible effectively in class unless the teacher makes it possible for him to do so. With all emphasis, we say that no Sunday school will ever function properly as a real Bible teaching school until each and every pupil owns a Bible, brings it to the Sunday school, and is led by the teacher to use it in the lesson period. One of the

richest contributions a Sunday school teacher can
make to the lives of his pupils is to put the Bible in
their hands and train them in using it.

4. *Secure Participation in Assemblies and Classes*

Each and every Sunday school pupil should be led
to participate in the department and school programs
as well as in the work of the class.

(1) *In the opening assembly*

Each pupil should have a songbook and be encouraged by teachers and class officers to sing.   He
should have his Bible and frequently be called upon
to engage in the responsive reading of the Scriptures.
The lesson text should not be read in the assembly.
Usually the program should be built around one or
more brief passages bearing on the lesson of the day.
This will encourage Bible reading and lesson study.

The habit of reading the Word of God in the department or the general assembly Sunday morning is
always helpful. It puts the Bible at the center. Nothing
should be allowed to crowd out the public reading of
the Scriptures in the Sunday school.

(2) *In gathering reports*

Here the teacher and class president have a fine
opportunity for helping the pupils.   Each member,
from Junior age up, should make up his own record
under the guidance of the teacher and class president.
This helps him to appreciate the value of the Six Point
Record System and to find out what each point means.
The correct use of the Six Point Record System will
prove a useful factor in the development of the pupil.

The spiritual benefits of the six habits involved in
the record system should be kept uppermost.   It will

be helpful frequently to have members, as they mark their records, repeat the Scriptures on which the six points are based. (See Information Card, Form 5).

(3) *In the lesson period*

During the lesson period the teacher should give each pupil an opportunity for self-expression. The knowledge which one gives out aids in his development more than that which he keeps to himself. Leading pupils to share learning activities is a far more effective method of teaching than is telling the lesson to the class.

Teachers may plan for their pupils to read the lesson text and Scriptures bearing on the lesson, recite from memory brief Scripture quotations, tell an appropriate Bible story, give from memory other illustrations, read a brief paper and in many ways take an active part in the lesson period. The teacher will always have to plan far ahead in order to have class members participate intelligently.

5. *Enlist in Scriptural Giving*

If Sunday school pupils are to be developed individually and helped in their spiritual lives, each and every one should make regular offerings to the support of the church's worldwide program. One of the finest spiritual exercises that one may enjoy is the act of contributing of his means to the support of the gospel. No pupil should be allowed to neglect this, and no Sunday school teacher has done his whole duty toward the spiritual development of his pupils until he has secured their participation in the church's budget. (See chapter 8).

The teacher is nearer to the pupil than any other worker in the church. He can promote the spiritual

development of all of his class members by leading
them to subscribe to the church budget and to contribute weekly of their means to the support of the
gospel.

6. *Encourage Preaching Attendance*

Some one will ask, Is attendance upon the preaching
service Sunday school work? What has this to do with
teaching the Bible in the Sunday school? Most as-
suredly it is Sunday school work of the highest order.

What is the Sunday school objective? It is the development of every member to the highest spiritual
attainment. Both the teaching of the Bible at the
Sunday school hour and the preaching of the gospel
immediately following are essential. The two are
complementary. They are interdependent, each helping the other and each reinforcing the other. The
teaching of the Word and the preaching of the Word
go hand in hand.

Sunday school teachers are warned against neglect-
ing for one moment to put their whole influence back
of the preaching service if they desire to make their
Sunday school function at its highest in developing
the lives of their pupils.

II. THE SCHOOL MUST BE PROPERLY ORGANIZED AND GRADED

If a Sunday school is to function effectively in
teaching the Bible and developing all the pupils individually along the lines we have been studying, it
must be thoroughly organized and properly graded.

1. *Thoroughly Organized*

Every Sunday school can and should have a sufficient
number of officers and teachers in the organization to

take care of the work adequately. This holds good in rural Sunday schools as well as in city Sunday schools.

The possibilities for the membership of the school, not its present enrolment, determine the size of the organization needed. Experience has proved that schools need to provide an average of at least one worker for every ten persons who should be enrolled. This average holds true in schools of all types everywhere. No matter how many officers and teachers the school needs, the organization should be maintained to its fullest capacity.

How often we see a small Sunday school with its organization limited to a superintendent and four or five other workers when it should have a full corps of general officers and a score or more teachers. Often the superintendent is not only directing the school, but is leading the music and is also teaching a class; the secretary is trying to fill several other offices, and each teacher has among his unenrolled prospects a sufficient number of pupils of different ages for several classes.

Lack of enough workers is the primary reason why nearly half of the churches in our Convention have Sunday schools enrolling less than one hundred people.

How often do we see a Sunday school which should provide for full departmentization limping along on a class basis. Other schools permit general officers to serve also as department officers, or perhaps use department officers as teachers.

Schools needing four or five departments for adults continue with only one or two. Classes are permitted to go without teachers for months at a time requiring combination with other classes Sunday after Sunday. As a result members all up and down the line gradually drop out of the school for lack of proper organization and leadership.

Sunday schools in which such conditions exist are not the exception at all. There are too many such schools. They cannot be good schools. Functioning in this manner, they are failing to give every pupil the things needed for his spiritual development.

The conditions described are not a necessity anywhere. They exist because pastors, superintendents, and other leaders do not study their work and put into their Sunday school the energy and business sense necessary to maintain a thorough organization. The leaders should open their eyes and lead the church to select and elect a full corps of officers and teachers, and to train them for their duties.

2. *Properly Graded*

When is a Sunday school properly graded? The answer is, When it is divided into groups in such a way as to minister equally to the spiritual needs of all the pupils. Another question arises, What basis then should be used in grading a Sunday school? In seeking for an answer to this, one thing is clear. If all the pupils are to be treated fairly and impartially, a single basis of grading must be observed.

When we consider that the spiritual needs of all the pupils are to be met and that a single basis for grading must be observed, it becomes clear that the most practical plan for grading a Sunday school is to use the age basis for all members, including adults.

All experience and observation teach that Sunday schools which try to follow different bases for grading are in a "hodge-podge," mixed pickle condition. They are not graded at all.

The wisdom of grading on an age basis has been fully proved by the results in growth and in effective Bible teaching seen in Southern Baptist Sunday schools during the past quarter of a century. This plan has made possible small classes which can minister to individual needs through lesson materials prepared especially for each age.

Experience has shown that age-grading is fully practical with adults as with other groups. Wherever Sunday school leaders have been willing to study the situation prayerfully, to educate the people patiently and lovingly, and then to pursue the plan of age-grading with firmness and tact, adults have responded. Many of our schools now have adult classes with less than a five-year range. The result in every case has been more men and women reached and better Bible study made possible.

II. THE OFFICERS MUST UNDERSTAND THEIR WORK AND DO IT

Good Sunday schools do not "just grow." They come about because the officers understand their work and do it.

1. *Accept Responsibility for Good Teaching*

Responsibility for good teaching in the Sunday school rests, first of all, upon the officers and it is imperative that they should train themselves for their duties. They cannot evade responsibility by claiming that trained teachers are the supreme need.

It has been truly said that "only trained soldiers are able to win hard battles." At the same time an army of perfectly trained soldiers becomes impotent under the leadership of incompetent, untrained officers.

The same principle applies in the business world. No enterprise can develop the best trained employees if there is not efficient management.

Of course, it requires trained soldiers to win battles, but it takes trained officers to lead a trained army to success. Of course, intelligent, courteous employees are essential to the success of every great business enterprise, but it requires an intelligent, vigorous management to develop and govern skilled employees. Of course, trained Sunday school teachers are necessary to the successful teaching of the Bible, but it requires consecrated, energetic, informed Sunday school officers to train, utilize and lead them if their services are to count for the most in the Sunday school.

Does this claim in any way weaken the emphasis that should be placed upon the importance of trained Bible teachers in the Sunday school? Not in the least. It places responsibility for developing good teachers in the Sunday school upon the officers, where it belongs.

2. *See That the School Is Well Conducted*

Sunday school teachers are far more dependent upon the manner in which the officers conduct the Sunday school than they realize. A corps of lifeless, uninformed Sunday school officers can handicap, embarrass, and cripple the work of fifty good teachers. An opinionated, indifferent superintendent has the same effect on a Sunday school organization that a log which has fallen across the highway has upon the automobile traffic. The Sunday school cannot make progress on account of him. It can neither go over him nor around him.

For a Sunday school to function properly as a Bible teaching agency and meet the individual needs of the members, it must be well conducted. The superintendent must direct things with intelligence, kindness, and gentleness but with the utmost firmness. He must be a thinker and a doer and "have a head of his own without being a mule."

3. *Plan Attractive Programs*

All Sunday schools whether they are organized on a class basis or on a department basis must offer helpful, pleasing assembly programs. It is practically impossible for a Sunday school even to approximate its highest efficiency in the teaching of the Word of God, no matter who the teachers are, if the superintendents do not make the assembly programs worth while.

Program-making is a skill which may be mastered by almost any one who will give it proper time and study. Personality and natural platform ability play a large part, but the ability to build a good program and present it attractively is achieved through constant study and practice.

A good program sets the stage for teaching the lesson and prepares both pupils and teachers in heart and mind for the classroom period. A good program, charmingly rendered, is a mighty factor in making the Sunday school an effective agency for teaching the Bible to all the pupils.

4. *Conduct Good Weekly Officers and Teachers' Meetings*

Certainly no Sunday school can ever achieve its best as a real Bible teaching agency unless it maintains a good weekly officers and teachers' meeting. A monthly workers' conference is no substitute for a weekly officers and teachers' meeting. The purpose of the two is different. One is for promotion mainly; the other has lesson preparation and improvement of teaching as a major feature. A weekly officers and teachers' meeting is an absolute necessity in securing the highest quality of work from all the officers and teachers in any Sunday school.

Why do not all Sunday schools have weekly officers and teachers' meetings? At least three things stand in the way. First, workers lack an understanding of what a real weekly officers and teachers' meeting is and what it will do for the Sunday school. Second, leaders are not willing to put into it the energy, time, and study necessary to make it go. Third, it costs money to maintain properly a good weekly officers and teachers' meeting, and the average finance committee, not knowing the value of such a meeting to the work, quibble over the expenditure of the necessary funds to make it a success.

Notwithstanding all this, whenever the pastor and superintendent make up their minds that they need a weekly officers and teachers' meeting and determine to have one, the church can be brought to support it, if it is made worth while. Likewise, the officers and teachers can be induced to attend when the meeting is put on the right basis, made attractive, and of practical help.

Without a good weekly officers and teachers' meeting, it is practically impossible for a Sunday school to function fully as a Bible teaching agency, giving to each and every pupil what he needs of the Word of God.

5. *Promote an Adequate Training Program*

Every church should have a well-defined plan and program for the training of its Sunday school workers. This program should be planned to run continuously throughout the year. It requires consecrated, intelligent, informed, trained men and women to make a good Sunday school.

Every church can have such workers, no matter where it is located, if it will get at the task in dead earnest. These trained officers and teachers are to be developed out of the raw material of which there is an abundant supply in each and every church.

It makes one faint at heart to hear pastors and super-intendents excusing their failures because they have no trained workers. One says, "Our people are a working class and haven't the ability or the time to take the necessary training."

Another says, "I'm pastor of a country church, and our people are not well enough educated to take the training."

Another says, "Our church is composed of factory people. There are not a half a dozen college graduates in the church. Therefore, they cannot be trained and developed into efficient Sunday school officers and teachers."

Still another says, "Our people are so worldly and so bent on business and social affairs that we cannot get them to take the training."

All these objections seem formidable. However, they are for the most part imaginary, and every one of them can be overcome in the "strength of the Lord and in the power of his might," and each and every Sunday school can be made to function as a great Bible teaching agency.

What is needed is a new attitude on the part of these leaders and a mastery of the plans of Southern Baptists for training their Sunday school officers and teachers. See chapter 5, this study.

6. *Use a Good System of Records*

If any Sunday school anywhere will have its officers and teachers thoroughly master the Six Point Record

System and put it into operation as recommended, it will do much to raise the grade of teaching done and to secure co-operation in all the school's affairs.

The Six Point Record System stands each pupil out to himself and tells the officers and teachers what that pupil does week after week and month after month. This information is essential to individual ministry by the teacher. It serves as a "habit meter" to give the standing of each individual in relation to the six important pupil activities incorporated in this system. Without this information Sunday school officers and teachers are largely working in the dark. Rightly used, the Six Point Record System is a powerful instrument to aid the teacher in the accomplishment of his task in teaching the Word of God.

When the administrative officers of the Sunday school —the pastor, superintendent, associate superintendents, secretary, department superintendents and their associates—master their work and attend to their duties as they should they can lead in an effective use of the records. They can develop the right kind of teachers, each trained for his particular task. They can build a real Bible teaching school able to minister to the spiritual needs of all the pupils individually. Then, and not until then, will Sunday schools function in the highest degree as Bible teaching agencies.

IV. THE TEACHER MUST BE A REAL BIBLE TEACHER

Having discussed the particular things the pupil should be led to do and the kind of school to which he should belong, we shall now discuss some fundamental things that should obtain in a teacher's life if he really teaches the Bible and gives to the members those things which are essential to their development.

1. *Appreciate the Sacredness of His Work*

The Sunday school teacher's work is a sacred commitment. It is a holy task. He is a real ambassador of the Lord Jesus, standing in Christ's stead, and praying men to become reconciled to God. Every winning Sunday school teacher must have something of this conception of his work or else he can never teach the Bible and claim the lives of his pupils for Christ as he should.

The Sunday school teacher should, in a large measure, be able to enter into the spirit of Paul and say, Woe is me if I fail to do my best with this Sunday school class—woe is me if I measure not up to Christ's expectations of me in this opportunity—woe is me if I fail to be a Sunday school teacher who teaches.

The worker who ministers to the individual needs of his pupils and makes good as a Bible teacher cannot approach his task lightly. He cannot regard as matters of convenience his constant, active interest in absent pupils; his constant preparation for his work; his regular, prompt attendance upon the sessions of the school and his regular attendance at the weekly officers and teachers' meeting. His Sunday school work must come first in the arrangement of his plans. Teaching in Sunday school is serious business and calls for the best in every one who undertakes it.

2. *Love People*

The only way we can possibly understand what it means to love people truly is to study Christ's attitude and conduct toward people. He visited them in their homes; he talked with them by the wayside; he mingled with the throngs and touched elbows with them in their everyday life; he preached to them and taught them at every opportunity; he fed the hungry multitudes; he made well the sick and healed the crippled; he mingled his tears with those who suffered; he was willing to spend and be spent for the unfortunate; he wept over the lost; he forgave the sins of the erring; he was patient at all times. Christ loved people.

If Sunday school teachers are ever to attain the highest success in their work; if they are ever to realize the greatest and fullest joys which await them, they must love people as Christ loved them. At least their love must be akin to the love of Christ.

How we do miss the joys that should be ours and fail to measure up to our Christ-given opportunities and exalted privileges as Sunday school teachers and Christian workers because we fail to let Christ manifest through us his love to those who need him! In the Scriptures we are enjoined to "keep ourselves in the love of God." This we may do by seeking at all times to minister to our members in loving, unselfish service.

3. *Desire to Learn*

One often hears these questions: How much time do you think a Sunday school teacher should give each week to the study of the lesson? How much time to special preparation, studying books on the Bible, methods of organization, methods of teaching and other study courses in preparing himself for his work? Of course, there can be no rule governing this matter. Love does not work by rules. Suffice it to say that Sunday school teachers must study regularly, constantly, and always. Jesus commanded us to "pray without ceasing." Just so, Sunday school teachers who win and develop their pupils spiritually as they should must study without ceasing.

Sunday school teachers are busy men and women. All of them have business, social, and home obligations.

However, they must set aside some time every day to study if they are to minister properly to the spiritual needs of their pupils.

It is not the province of this brief word about the Sunday school teacher to tell what he should study or to catalogue a list of subjects and books. These are on every hand and may be secured by teachers everywhere. Pamphlets listing books in the Sunday School Training Course may be secured from the Sunday School Department, Baptist Sunday School Board, Nashville 3, Tennessee.

After the class discussion on this chapter use Section II of the workbook in the appendix for review.

CHAPTER III

THE SUNDAY SCHOOL FUNCTIONING AS AN EMPLOYMENT AGENCY

Pastors are generally agreed that one of the outstanding needs of the churches today is to keep all the members constantly busy at worth-while tasks.

I. GOD INTENDS THAT EVERY ONE OF HIS CHILDREN SHALL BE BUSY

The New Testament calls the church the Body of Christ and teaches that the health of this spiritual body requires that every member shall function.

1. *All Christians Should Be Workers*

Certainly, little argument is needed to convince one that every child of God should be busy every day about the Father's business. Jesus set an example to his followers by living an intensely busy life. The Apostles and early followers of Jesus threw themselves into the channels of service with unstinted zeal and burning fervor.

The Scriptures abound in urgent appeals to God's children to get busy and keep busy about his work. In fact, the entire New Testament is filled with passages containing admonitions of this kind. Also, the Scriptures in many places characterize Christians as "workmen" and "laborers." Certainly if the followers of Jesus are to fulfil their mission in carrying forward the work that Jesus began, they must be busy every day.

For example, in 1 Corinthians 3:9 the disciples of

Christ are called "God's fellow-workers" (ASV). In James 1:22-24, they are enjoined to be doers of the Word and not hearers only. Paul admonished Timothy, "Give diligence to present thyself approved unto God, a workman that needeth not to be ashamed" (2 Tim. 2:15 ASV).

There is no need to multiply Scripture quotations further to convince one that every child of God is saved to serve. His service bears testimony to the fact that he has been saved.

A veritable army of unemployed Christians, holding membership in our churches, need to be put to work. They have talent, they have ability, and in the heart of every one there is a God-given desire to serve Christ. The difficulty is they do not know what to do. They need some one to assign them suitable tasks and guide and encourage them in doing the work.

The present situation is clearly set out in the parable of the laborers in the vineyard (Matt. 20:1-6). If unemployed Christians were approached today with the question, "Why stand ye here all the day idle?" from the innermost part of their souls they would answer, "No man hath hired us, we do not know what to do."

As one gazes upon the great army of unemployed church members, he might be led to believe that there is either nothing for them to do or they have not been saved. But neither of these assumptions is true. Perhaps there are some people in all churches who have been mistaken about their conversion, but the number is negligible as compared with the great multitude of true believers in Christ.

The fact is, when people are converted they are babes in Christ. They do not know what to do and their greatest need is for somebody to provide for them tasks which they can do, and to help and encourage them until they get a good start along the pathway of service. It is false reasoning to say that they cannot serve until they have grown in Christian experience. Jesus used the twelve when they were yet immature.

Neither are Christians idle because there is not work for all to do. The need is for somebody to bring the work and the workers together. Bible teaching is not complete until the learners have found channels through which to practice the truth.

2. *Plenty of Work to Be Done*

There is plenty of work to do. On every hand there is sin, sickness, sorrow, ignorance, discouragement, weakness, hopelessness, death! The fields are white! White!! White!!! The crying need is for every child of God to be enlisted in unselfish, definite service doing the things that Christ did when he was on earth and which he enjoined upon us to do. The burning question of the hour is, "How may pastors and churches utilize effectively the great host of idle members in all the churches in meeting the needs that are so apparent all around us?"

Every idle Christian is a liability on the pastor's hands and an added burden on his heart. Something must be done to remedy this deplorable situation and convert every one of these idle church members into useful workers for Christ. The question arises, How may this be done? Where may worthy, suitable tasks for so many unemployed church members be found? The answer is, In the Sunday school.

II. Places of Service for All in the Sunday School

The tasks are numerous and varied. The organization of a growing Sunday school requires a large personnel. We have seen that one of the most frequent weaknesses is the failure of churches to provide an adequate corps of workers. Yet in every church there are persons suited to every task. The gifts of the members are as varied and different as the needs. "Unto each one of us was the grace given according to the measure of the gift of Christ" (Eph. 4:7 ASV). "And he gave some to be apostles; and some, prophets; and some, evangelists; and some, pastors and teachers" (Eph. 4:11 ASV).

As it was in New Testament times, so it is today. In all our churches we have capable people of varied gifts and talents who, if enlisted and trained, will be able to do valiant service for Christ. Let us see how all these may be utilized in a practical way through service in our Sunday schools.

1. *Some Have Executive Ability*

In every church there are men and women and young people of outstanding executive ability, capable of leadership in business, social and civic affairs. These same gifts may be used in a fine way in places of executive leadership in the Sunday school. The pastor and superintendent should analyze the church roll carefully and select the men and women best suited to be officers of the Sunday school. Each one should be selected for a place because of his willingness and capacity to become proficient in that phase of the work.

In even the smallest Sunday schools there is need for a general superintendent, one or more associate superintendents, a secretary, chorister, pianist, and a church librarian.

Every school needs at least two department superintendents, one for the Cradle Roll and one for the Extension department. Teachers must function as administrators in guiding class activities. The class organization furnishes opportunities for Christians to serve and to gain experience which will fit them for larger service.

In schools with the minimum of nine departments some forty or more department officers will be needed. Where there are multiple departments for each age group, many more places of service are provided.

Each class above Primary age will have its own officers. The organization for Juniors will be simple, while officers of Young People's and Adult classes will carry much of the responsibility for the activities of the classes.

Thus we see that in a Sunday school which is properly and fully organized, there is ample opportunity for using a host of men and women with executive ability.

For each one of the general officers, each officer in any of the departments and each class officer there is a free pamphlet setting forth the duties. There are some sixty or seventy different pamphlets presenting the duties of those responsible for administration in the various units of a Sunday school. These are available from your state Sunday School secretary, or from the Sunday School Department, Baptist Sunday School Board, Nashville 3, Tennessee.

The Sunday School Training Course offers books on administration which present methods that have come out of prayer and experience. These methods have proved their value under all circumstances, where they have been wholeheartedly used by the Sunday school workers, in dependence upon the power and direction of the Holy Spirit.

2. *Some Have Teaching Gifts*

Few Sunday schools in the Southern Baptist Convention have enough teachers to care for the pupils who should attend. This is the main reason why the majority of our Sunday schools are not any larger.

In all our churches there are large numbers of men and women with potential teaching gifts and qualifications who have not been put to work. Leaders hesitate to enlist them in service and assign them to the task of teaching for the reason that they have never taught and are not "experts." Pastors and superintendents should select from the church roll all the men and women who, in their judgment, possess the ability to develop into good teachers. These should be enlisted in the training program and led to continuous effort to prepare themselves for effective service.

At the same time, a study should be made of the entire Sunday school organization to determine where additional teachers are needed. Many Sunday schools having ten teachers should have twenty-five; others having twenty should have fifty; others having fifty should have one hundred; and still others having one hundred should have two hundred or more. Nursery workers and visitors in the Cradle Roll and Extension departments are really teachers and should be so considered.

It will require faith and courage to set up new classes and other units to take care of people not yet enrolled in the Sunday school. But the results will advance the kingdom of God, not only in increased enrolment and attendance, but also in the spiritual development of the army of newly enlisted teachers and officers.

3. *Some Have Ability to Do Clerical Work*

Every Sunday school, to do its best work, must have a first-class system of records properly installed and correctly operated. For Southern Baptists, the Six Point Record System meets this need admirably. To operate this system in a Sunday school organized on the class basis, a general secretary and two associates are needed.   Added to these will be secretaries for the Cradle Roll and the Extension departments and for the classes above Primary age.

In larger Sunday schools, besides the general secretary and associates, there is a need for department secretaries with an associate for each.   The number of class secretaries needed may vary from about twenty to some two hundred or more.

Thus we see that the operation of a first-class system of records provides service opportunities for an army of alert, vigorous Christians of varying ages.   They should understand that their ministry is as much a spiritual matter as that of the teachers and they should be trained for their work and encouraged to do it in the best possible way.

The Sunday School Department of the Baptist Sunday School Board, Nashville 3, Tennessee, offers free pamphlets on the duties of the various secretaries. *The Six Point Record System and Its Use* by Noland, presents a fuller discussion.

4. *Many Can Visit in the Interest of the Sunday School*

How little do we appreciate the value of personal visitation in the service of Christ!   The fact is, personal contact with people whom we wish to help is the best way possible to reach them.   And it is difficult to measure the value which personal visitation in the interest of the Sunday school has for those who do the visiting.

New pupils need to be won for the Sunday school. There is just one effective way of winning them, and that is by personal visitation.   It is more than probable that if every one of our Sunday schools would maintain systematic, enthusiastic visitation for new pupils week by week that the attendance would be doubled inside of twelve months. In fact, the attendance of many would be doubled within one month's time.

Absent pupils need to be brought back. Purging Sunday school rolls by dropping the names of pupils who are indifferent and who do not attend regularly is sinful and should not be tolerated for a moment. On the contrary, systematic, persistent, constant visitation should be inaugurated and maintained in the interest of absent pupils.

Such visitation calls for organized effort, and provides a place of service for practically every Christian who is not a shut-in.

The associate superintendent in charge of enlargement will direct the visitation program of the entire school, working through the associates in the departments. These department officers will, in turn, make assignments to the classes and direct the visitation through their contacts in the weekly officers and teachers' meetings. They will hold special conferences to train and guide the vice presidents in charge of membership in the classes.

In classes for Young People and Adults, the membership vice presidents will work with and through the group captains. The aim will be not only to see that all absentees and prospects are visited, but also to see that every Christian gains the spiritual development which comes from participating in the visitation.

Face to face contacts should be emphasized. Telephone calls, letters, and post cards sent to absent pupils may represent time wasted, or worse. Sometimes these methods are simply alibis for real service. They have only limited value in Sunday school building.

If pastors, superintendents, department superintendents, and teachers would get busy, they could lead a host of enthusiastic Sunday school members in every community, every week, to visit in the interest of new pupils and absentees. They would thereby do a service which would produce glorious results in the lives of hundreds of people.

5. *Some May Carry Comfort to the Sick and Needy*

In every church there are people especially gifted in carrying comfort and joy to those who are sick and needy. Every church through its Sunday school organization may guide Christians into this loving personal service.

The Extension department of the Sunday school is especially fitted to locate these needy ones and to bring joy, gladness, consolation and help to them. A well-organized Extension department should have enough workers to keep under surveillance every home in the territory of the church. The pastor has in this body of fine men and women a real aid for intimate contact with the needy in the community.

An Extension department in an average sized church could provide places of service for ten or more workers. Free pamphlets on the work of this department may be secured from the Sunday School Department, Baptist Sunday School Board, Nashville 3, Tennessee, or from your state headquarters.

6. *Some Have Talents for Directing Social Activities*

The importance of the social life of a church must be recognized. All people, both old and young, are naturally social. The recreational activities in which they engage have large bearing upon their spiritual development and zeal for service.

It is a fact that one's social practices and habits are a fair index to his spiritual condition. A Christian cannot be wrong in his social habits and at the same time enjoy close and sweet fellowship with Christ. He cannot engage in questionable worldly pleasures and maintain a deep interest in things spiritual. His love for Christ will grow cold. His love for lost people and his power to win them to Christ will desert him.

Since this is true, how important it is that the churches should give the most careful and prayerful consideration to a well-planned program of social activities! The Sunday school lends itself to the promotion of the social life of its members. Grouping the pupils into classes and departments makes it easy to have enthusiastic class and department spirit as well as to generate a school spirit.

General direction of the social life of a Sunday school should be assigned to an associate superintendent with gifts for leading this phase of Christian activity. Serving with him, there should be in each department an associate superintendent in charge of fellowship. In the younger age-groups the department superintendent will usually serve in this capacity.

In each class above the Junior age the planning of the social life should be assigned to a class officer. In the younger age groups teachers should be charged with directing the social life of the different classes.

The various officers in charge of fellowship should function every Sunday to maintain a spirit of friendliness throughout the school. They are responsible for the attractiveness of the rooms. They should see that all who come are made to feel welcome and at home. They are also responsible for the social activities of the various classes and departments, in line with the church program.

In directing the whole program of social events, the associate superintendent in charge should work in closest co-operation with the pastor, superintendent, and other officers to co-ordinate the social life of the Sunday school and church. A schedule for the year will be prepared, showing dates for socials for all the church organizations.

Many schools will wish to hold at least one general social event, perhaps an annual picnic, to include all members of the Sunday school and congregation. If this is done, care must be exercised to provide graded recreational activities to meet the needs of all ages.

No small part of the social life of a church is provided through the fellowship at the weekly officers and teachers' meeting; the class business meetings, the parent-worker meetings, and other such gatherings.

The development of the sense of "together-ness" is closely akin to spiritual growth, and every individual who serves in any capacity to increase fellowship with other Christians in the church is rendering a spiritual service.

Helps in planning social activities may be secured through the books on church recreation featured in the *Church Library Booklist*. Some of these should be in your church library. The Baptist Book Store in your state can supply accepted books on church recreation and how to provide it.

7. *Some Have Special Musical Talents*

Good music is an absolute essential to the best work of a Sunday school. A great many people have special musical gifts which ought to be cultivated and used for Christ's glory. Every church through its Sunday school may use in a fine way those with musical ability.

Special attention should be given to those young people who have good voices and those who are able to play various musical instruments. This is one of the best ways to interest young people in the Sunday school.

Department superintendents should be talent scouts to discover and utilize the abilities of their members. Special music and other features in the assembly programs should be provided by the members of that department. The practice of bringing in outside talent is to be avoided unless for some exceptional reason.

The free literature on Sunday school work includes pamphlets dealing with the music for each department. In addition, the Department of Church Music, Baptist Sunday School Board, Nashville 3, Tennessee, offers helpful material for the improvement of the music in all units of church organization.

8. *All Should Be Soul-Winners*

In Sunday school the pastor has practically all the soul-winners in the church, and through it he may reap the greatest harvest of souls. In the Sunday school every saved pupil, teacher, and officer may find an opportunity for real work as a soul-winner.

The pastor and the general superintendent working together may infuse a soul-winning spirit into the whole church life. Through the Sunday school organization it is the most practical matter in the world to enlist the members in soul-winning.

First, the general superintendent is charged with winning every lost person in the Sunday school. Next each department superintendent is charged with winning the lost in his particular department. And then each teacher should accept the responsibility of winning every lost pupil in his class. With the aid of class officers who are dedicated Christians, teachers will find it possible to inspire every saved pupil to put forth earnest efforts to win his fellow pupils who do not know Christ.

We have in all churches a great host of saved people, each and every one of whom could and should be an earnest soul-winner. The Sunday school when properly organized and operated brings this host of saved people into service and puts each one in contact with lost people.

9. *Every Church Member Should Be Enlisted*

Pastors and superintendents should earnestly study the great question of "human adjustment." With the guidance of the Holy Spirit they should apply this fine art in the assignment of suitable tasks to scores of idle church members who are capable of rendering effective service for Christ in the Sunday school.

With proper executive leadership any Sunday school in any church can be so organized that a place of useful, joyous service may be made for every member of the church.

Turn to Section III of the workbook in the appendix for guidance in summarizing this chapter.

CHAPTER IV

THE SUNDAY SCHOOL FUNCTIONING AS AN OUTREACHING AGENCY

In order to do its work most effectively, every church should have certain definite information concerning the conditions, needs, and possibilities of the field to be touched directly by its ministry. This knowledge the church must have if it would carry out a vigorous teaching, preaching, and soul-winning program. Let us consider some of the things a church should know about the field.

I. THE SIZE OF THE FIELD

To be sure the field is the world to every Baptist church. However, there is also a "Jerusalem" for every church. It is the contigious territory which that church should work like a garden.

1. *Legitimate Area*

In country communities, distance and accessibility largely determine the area to be included. In towns, frequently the corporate limits are allowed to serve as boundary lines. In cities where there is more than one Baptist church generally the pastors and churches agree as to the boundary lines circumscribing the active field of operation for each church.

Of course each church will determine the limits of its own Jerusalem. But many churches have restricted themselves to a territory which is too small. There should be no unreached areas between the churches.

If any church finds that it cannot minister to the people in the territory stretching out in all directions half-way to the next Baptist church, then new work should be started. Usually this will be done through branch Sunday schools. Great Southern Baptist mission fields lie in the neglected areas between churches.

2. *Number of People Available*

The area of its field does not determine the real size of a church's possibilities for service. The number of people who dwell in that field determines this important matter. Intelligent provision in at least two major matters depends on a church's knowledge of the number of people living in its local field.

(1) *The organization needed*

It is a foolish policy for a church to maintain a Sunday school organization only large enough to minister to the needs of the people already enrolled.

The number of people available in the church's field, instead of the size of the church membership or the present Sunday school enrolment must determine the size and kind of organization the church should maintain. In the business world men build their organizations in view of what they consider their legitimate possibilities for business. Churches should do the same.

The number of unreached possibilities for a Sunday school may be as great as the number of people already on the church roll and the Sunday school roll combined. Many churches are operating small class Sunday schools when potentially their fields justify full department organizations. The churches need to inform themselves concerning the number to be reached and provide an average of at least one worker for every ten people they aim to enrol in the Sunday school.

(2) The kind of building and equipment to provide

The size and kind of building a church erects determines not only the character of the work the church does but also the magnitude of its operations.

Except for a few of the recently completed buildings, the majority of church houses are too small. They were erected to take care of the existing Sunday school and the congregation attending the preaching services at the time the building was erected. They were not planned with a view of providing a place for every man, woman, and child available in the church's territory.

In preparing to erect a new building, the church should plan to take care of all the people available in its legitimate local field. This can be done with accuracy only as a church has a knowledge of the number of people residing in this field, and of the population trends to be expected.

II. The Personnel of the Field

It is not enough for a church simply to know how many people dwell within the confines of its legitimate territory. Christianity is a personal matter. The Gospel writers so emphasize it. Jesus called the twelve one by one, and no doubt the seventy were selected in the same way. The Gospel writers speak of "a certain man," "a certain woman," "a young man," "a little girl," "a centurion's servant." Jesus did not generalize but gave all his messages extremely practical applications to individual situations.

Just so, if our pastors and churches would be highly effective they must deal with people individually. In order to do this they should have certain definite knowledge of each person within the confines of the territory of the church.

1. *The Lost People*

The name of every man, woman, and child in the community who is a stranger to grace should be in the possession of the church and the pastor. It is very much easier to become intensely concerned about the salvation of the souls of people when we know them personally, who they are and where they live.

Bill Smith may be only one of a hundred lost people in the community. However, the chances of winning Bill Smith to Christ are multiplied a hundredfold when we have his name, age, and address, and know from his own testimony that he is a lost man.

2. *The Unaffiliated Baptists*

The great army of "detached" Baptists that we hear so much about can be greatly reduced. If every pastor and church will learn the names of all unaffiliated Baptists in their territory and then go after these people vigorously they can be led to join the church and put themselves and their means in position to be used.

3. *The Sick and Needy*

By all means our churches ought to minister to the sick and the destitute. Christ would have us do this. However, we will not perform this ministry unless we know who these people are, where they live, and the peculiar needs of each. This information churches must seek continuously for the use of the pastor and others able to minister to these needy people.

III. The Church Using Its Sunday School as an Outreaching Agency

The church may utilize the Sunday school not only to secure and make available the needed information,

but also to reach out in ministry to those for whom
the church is responsible.

1. *Conducting a Religious Census*

The idea of a religious census has been discussed so
often that a lengthy presentation of the subject is not
needed here. However, churches sometimes take a
religious census and receive very little benefit from it.
Often the fault lies in the manner in which the census
was taken. Sometimes failure comes because the information was not properly prepared for use. Still more
often, the church fails to follow up the census, and so
the information is laid aside and never used. A census
correctly taken, properly prepared for use, and vigorously followed up will produce large benefits and bring
untold blessings to many lives.

The use of a religious census for the purpose of securing certain definite information about the people residing in the community contigious to the church house
is an absolute necessity, if the church would minister
to all the people. No other method is equal to it.

A census should be taken at least annually in every
situation. In industrial and manufacturing centers and
rapidly growing sections, two to four times each year
is not too frequent. In mill communities and other
places, where the population changes often, a census
may be needed more frequently, unless there is provision for keeping the records up to date.

The kind of census we are discussing is taken by the
Sunday school organization and the information gained
is primarily for the use of building the Sunday school.
The directions for taking it and for tabulating the
information are given with the Sunday school in mind.
At the same time the information may be used by the
church and pastor in serving a much wider purpose.

For a correct method for taking and using a census, the reader is referred to chapter 3 in *Building a Standard Sunday School.*

2. *Reaching Out After the People*

Prepare the Sunday school to go into action to reach the people. It is time to quit quibbling and dillydallying and get out into the homes and the places of business and urge people to join the Sunday school and attend the services of worship.

We no longer need to experiment with ways to reach the people. We know the steps which work every where: (1) find the people, (2) provide space, (3) enlarge the organization, (4) train the workers, (5) maintain systematic visitation.

Pastors and churches are confronted with small Sunday schools, and the congregations at the services of worship are pitiably small. What is needed is for the Sunday school organizations to be increased to an immeasurable degree, instructed and sent out into the community round about that the people may be "compelled" to attend the services.

When this is done the cry that people have lost interest in the churches will cease; the cry that churches are dead and dying will no longer be heard. Every church has in its Sunday school a powerful outreaching agency which, if used intelligently and constantly, will work a transformation in any situation no matter how hopeless it may appear.

3. *Maintaining Regular Visitation*

The Sunday school teachers and pupils should keep in touch with the field by constant visitation in the homes. Every Sunday school should observe a regular visitation program. Nothing else will take its place.

In Sunday school visitation those who go are frequently seeking to reach new pupils and to bring back absentees. However, each visitor should be alert to gather information regarding all unenrolled members of every family. He should be in search of any information which will assist the pastor and church in ministering to both the physical and spiritual needs of the people.

Visitors should keep a sharp lookout for new people moving into the community, for cases of sickness, for people in distress and trouble and for those who are lost and sin-sick.

On one occasion, a teacher and two Junior girls were visiting absentees and prospective pupils for their class. In passing a residence they noticed a moving van unloading. They stopped and made inquiry of a gentleman and found he was moving in from another city. The information was reported immediately to the Sunday school superintendent.

The family consisted of father and mother and two children, all of whom joined the Sunday school the following Sunday. The father, mother, and one of the children joined the church. The father and mother immediately accepted positions as Sunday school teachers.

The man had been superintendent of the Sunday school and his wife a teacher of a young ladies' class in the church from which they came. They were not out of fellowship or service even one day all because they were promptly discovered by Sunday school visitors.

Two Intermediate workers were visiting in the interest of absentees and new pupils. In conversation with a mother whose daughter they were seeking for the Sunday school, they learned that her next-door neighbors were not Christians and that none of the family attended services anywhere.

The workers called, and on being admitted to the house, they found an aged grandmother, her daughter, and several small children, not one of whom was a professing Christian. The workers read the Bible, pressed the claims of Jesus upon their hearts, prayed for and with them, and won both the grandmother and her daughter to Christ. They also secured full information regarding each member of the family. Based on this information, visitation assignments were made to each department and class responsibile for any person in the home.

Any number of illustrations could be given where detached church members, sick and destitute people, and people without Christ, have been discovered, helped, and blessed because of the visits of godly workers.

All the information gained by Sunday school visitors should be passed on to the superintendents, who should digest it, give to the pastor such information as he should have, and see that every department and class receives its information without delay.

IV. METHODS OF ACCOMPLISHING VISITATION

It is not enough to urge everybody to visit. Pastors and superintendents must accept the responsibility for planning a visitation program, of maintaining the organization needed, and of training and inspiriting the workers.

1. *Monthly Visitation Day*

Every Sunday school should observe visitation day at least once a month for the purpose of reaching both absent and prospective pupils. In rural communities the last Sunday in each month may prove to be the best time.   In many town and city churches Saturday afternoon preceding the first Sunday in each month has been found to be an acceptable time.

In large schools, each department may decide upon the day and hour best suited to its constituency. But there should be a definite time each month.

All the pupils absent the previous Sundays and many prospective pupils for the Sunday school should be visited by representatives of the department or class involved.

2. *Regular Weekly Visitation*

Every absent pupil should be visited some time during the week following his absence.   In this way will absent pupils be impressed with the fact that the Sunday school is interested in them.   In this way can the class rolls be kept up-to-date. In this way can the interest of teachers and pupils be maintained in irregular pupils and in the Sunday school as a whole.

3. *Special Department and Class Visitation*

Frequently, it is advisable for a department or a class to put on an intensive visitation campaign.   The visitors may meet at the church building in the evening about six-thirty and from there go into the homes of irregular pupils and those who should be new members for the Sunday school.   Where the absentees and prospects may be seen in their places of business, the visiting may be done in the afternoons.

4. *Assignments and Reports*

As a general thing, personal workers and visitors should go in pairs.   Usually they should work on the basis of information furnished them from the results of a religious census. The assignments should be made on regular Six Point Record forms, which should be properly filled out and returned immediately to those directing the visitation.

Several forms are offered. These should be studied and used according to the need.

Form 105. General Visitation Assignment and Report. This has space for information about the person to be visited, guidance as to the purpose, and space for reporting the results. It magnifies visitation for various spiritual ministries in addition to securing enrolment and attendance.

Form 110. Absentee Visitation and Assignment Report. This has space for the information needed by the one who visits an absentee, and for the report of the results of each visit.

Form 120. Prospect Visitation Assignment and Report. This is similar to Form 110, except that it is used to assign visitation of prospective members, and to report progress in enlisting them.

The weekly officers and teachers' meeting offers the best opportunity for making assignments and receiving reports. The workers should be trained in how to visit, and how to get and report definite results.

The responsibility for maintaining a program of visitation should be placed upon the teachers and officers. They should be led to see that Bible study is not complete until it has sent the members out in ministry to others.

5. *Taking Christ to the People*

The discussion thus far has emphasized visitation to secure new members and bring back absentees. But we must never lose sight of the fact that the visitor going in the name of Christ has as his objective ministry to each individual according to his needs.

(1) *Personal work with the lost*

When Jesus was on earth he did not wait for the people to come to the house of worship. The apostles during the early days of Christianity went everywhere preaching, teaching, and speaking to the people, on the streets, by the roadside, and in their homes.

Of course, it is utterly impossible for a pastor to do all this work himself, but he has a Sunday school organization composed of dedicated men and women whom he may use for this purpose. Any pastor, no matter how large his church, may use his Sunday school organization for visiting regularly in every home in the confines of his church territory.

Sunday school workers should visit the people in their homes for the purpose of speaking to them about their souls and their church affiliation. They should minister to the sick and needy. They should visit to encourage lesson preparation, systematic giving, attendance at preaching, and all the habits promoted by the record system. They should seek to minister to the entire family as opportunity affords, keeping in mind the objective: A Christian home for every member of our Sunday school.

(2) *Fellowship with the shut-ins*

In this connection, John C. Carlisle, in *Baptist Times*, says "Under the shadow of the churches, in lonely rooms there are those who are prisoners of pain. They have been shut off from their fellows by the infirmities of age. It is not possible for them to unite in public worship. They have to be sought out. They do not

send asking for visitors, they would be surprised if any-
one called to see them.

"Yet it should be the business of each Christian community to provide some fellowship for the sick and the
suffering. It is not a question of charity, but of contact. Those who have the strength and the knowledge
must recognize that they are debtors to the weak and
the ignorant.

"A friendly call or a word of cheer might mean so
much, and it costs so little. It is invaluable in the new
spirit it introduces, not only in the church but in the
individual. We may render help to others and in so
doing we are sure to obtain help for ourselves. In keeping his commandments there is great reward."

While the Extension department has a wonderful
ministry to shut-ins, all Christians need to have the
experience of sharing love and cheer with those who
need it.

(3) *Ministry to the indifferent*

It is true that many people seem negligent about their
spiritual condition. Their interest in their church relationship is at low ebb. The pleasures and cares of the
world cause a neglect of the spiritual life. Great multitudes of people, rich and poor alike, have always been
pleasure mad. Likewise the cares of the world, house-
hold affairs and business pursuits—things legitimate in
themselves—have proved effective loadstones to drag
people away and cause them to forget God's claim upon
their lives.

The cravings of the natural heart have ever been
at variance to man's spiritual interest. The devil, man's
arch enemy, has ever been alert to drag him down into
shame, disgrace, and even death.

Many persons who desire to become active Christians are deterred because of preconceived notions about churches and church members. It is too true that some churches are cold, formal, and powerless in their services. Some church members are stiff and inhospitable and even godless in their lives. At the same time a vast majority of professing Christians love Christ and hate sin and are deeply concerned about the souls of their fellow men.

Those who are on the outside are too ready to magnify the faults and frailties of our churches and church members and use these in justification of their own conduct. Whatever the causes of spiritual negligence, they can best be removed by loving, Spirit-directed visitation.

6. *Utilizing All Christians*

The Lord calls upon all Christians to visit and speak to people about Christ, to comfort the needy, to bring cheer to the homes of the sick, and to woo the indifferent. The pastor is only the leader and overseer in this Christlike mission.

Visiting was the responsibility of all Christians in New Testament times and it must be now if we are going to do it Christ's way and win the multitudes to him.

Any church, no matter how lifeless it may seem, can be reconstructed spiritually if the pastor will lead his Sunday school officers, teachers, and pupils in prayerful, earnest, house-to-house visitation.

By using this method constantly and enthusiastically, any church anywhere can more than fill its valuable space with the Sunday school pupils and overflow the auditorium with worshipers at the eleven o'clock hour.

Multitudes of precious souls will be won to Christ, and songs of joy and praise will ascend daily to God.

Let us hearken to the words of Christ and see what he says about this, and then do it in his way.

"Then shall the King say unto them on his right hand, Come, ye blessed of my Father, inherit the kingdom prepared for you from the foundation of the world: for I was hungry, and ye gave me to eat; I was thirsty, and ye gave me drink; I was a stranger, and ye took me in; naked, and ye clothed me; I was sick, and ye visited me; I was in prison, and ye came unto me. Then shall the righteous answer him, saying, Lord, when saw we thee hungry, and fed thee? or athirst, and gave thee drink? And when saw we thee a stranger, and took thee in? or naked, and clothed thee? And when saw we thee sick, or in prison, and came into thee? And the King shall answer and say unto them, Verily, I say unto you, Inasmuch as ye did it unto one of these my brethren, even these least, ye did it unto me" (Matt. 25:34-40 ASV).

After the class discussion on this chapter, turn to the appendix and use Section IV of the workbook for review and application.

CHAPTER V

THE SUNDAY SCHOOL FUNCTIONING AS A CHURCH TRAINING AGENCY

The Sunday school is commonly thought of in connection with teaching the Bible, and the Training Union with training for service. However, one has only to give the briefest consideration to the training program which every church may and should put on through its Sunday school organization to be convinced of the important place the Sunday school may fill as a church training agency.

The nature of the training done through the Sunday school correlates with that done by the Training Union. Much of it deals with a more limited constituency in that it is addressed to officers, teachers, and prospective workers.

The courses of the two organizations are integrated in the fields of Bible study, doctrines, and evangelism. Both seek to reach all church members for study of books in these areas. When the Sunday school organization is properly used as a church training agency, it supplements the work of the Training Union and offers a marvelous opportunity for the training of church members along the lines of useful, practical service.

I. EVERY CHURCH MUST TRAIN AND DEVELOP ITS ENTIRE MEMBERSHIP

It is absolutely imperative that every church train and develop its entire membership if church members are to become highly useful in any line of Christian service. We sometimes make the claim that people are "naturally" Baptists. However, they are not "naturally" informed Baptists. They cannot "naturally" take up any line of church work and go forward with it successfully. They must be trained.

1. *All Need Specific Training*

All church members need specific training. They need it in every phase of useful Christian service. To be a useful deacon requires that a man must have special training for his work as a deacon. Sunday school officers require training along distinctive lines. The same applies to Sunday school teachers and all other church workers.

Nor does it follow that a man or woman who is successful in his chosen profession or business can be highly successful in any phase of church work without making a specific study of that particular line of work. The work is different and each worker must be trained for his particular task. Just here lies one of our greatest problems in doing church work and at this point we meet some of our most serious obstacles.

A few familiar illustrations will serve in bringing this forcibly to our minds. A successful banker is elected to the office of deacon. He assumes that because he understands the banking business, he also understands the duties of the work of a deacon and sees no need that he should put himself in training for these duties.

A successful merchant is chosen superintendent of the Sunday school. He concludes that because he is a success as a merchant, he is therefore equipped to direct successfully the destinies of the Sunday school and refuses to put himself in training for his duties as superintendent.

Often successful secular school teachers are elected to teach the Bible in the Sunday school. Because of their efficiency and success in their secular school work, they assume that they are also prepared for teaching the Bible, and seem not to realize that they must have specific preparation and constantly keep themselves in training for their duties as teachers in the Sunday school.

An experienced bank cashier, accountant, or book-keeper is elected secretary of the Sunday school. He assumes, because of his standing in the business world and because of his extensive office experience, that he also knows all about the business of Sunday school bookkeeping. He fails to understand that the method of keeping Sunday school records is necessarily different from that applied to any other system of bookkeeping since its aims are distinctive.

He is likely to miss the spiritual aspects and objectives of the Six Point Record System. As a result, he changes certain forms and discontinues others to suit his own notions, thus largely nullifying the value of the record system.

What each and all of these workers need is to realize that church work is different from other kinds of work, and that every Christian who has been intrusted with leadership in any phase of church work needs to be trained for his duties.

The members of the church can be trained to do effective work. They are the same people who are leaders in the secular world. They are the successful farmers, skilled mechanics, expert doctors, successful lawyers, trained school teachers, outstanding professional men, successful housekeepers, expert office women, and leaders in the business affairs of the communities. The majority of these church members love the Lord and cherish a desire in their hearts to be of use in the kingdom. They are successful in their chosen vocations, and if properly adjusted and trained, each for his particular task, they will prove equally successful as church workers.

2. *Training Others for Christian Service Is an Art*

The one who leads in the training program of the Sunday school must have patience, perseverance, sympathy, and skill of a high order. The training process is long and painstaking. People must be led to exercise the patience required to continue.

The one who leads must deal with people individually, studying the particular and peculiar needs of each, working with unflagging zeal and buoyant faith, hoping for the best even when the outcome seems doubtful. Underneath all his efforts there must be a genuine love for people—a love akin to the Christ-love.

The Sunday school should elect a Spirit-filled Christian to be its associate superintendent in charge of training. He, with the associates in the departments, will keep a record of the training accomplished by each worker. This will enable him to give intelligent guidance to each one. He will maintain a training program based on the needs of his Sunday school. Cards for individual training records are offered by the Baptist Sunday School Board.

It is said that one of our largest manufacturers of toilet goods, soap, and perfumes has a rule which prohibits the employment of any one from outside their organization except at the bottom of the salary scale. All the positions requiring skilled labor are filled by those who have been developed and trained in the business. They claim that a business which cannot develop and train all the expert help it needs cannot attain the greatest success.

This is a good lesson for churches. They have plenty of first-class "raw material" going to waste for lack of culture and use. Every church should earnestly get at the work of utilizing, training, and developing its own members, for by so doing it will soon have skilled workers in charge of every phase of the church's activities.

II. Two Types of Training Essential

Developing an adequate number of trained workers is a task of tremendous proportions and requires a farsighted program including at least two essential types of training.

1. *The Study of Textbooks*

Theory is acquired through the study of textbooks. This method of educating and developing informed, effective workers in Christ's service is absolutely necessary. Church members who will not study the courses treating the different phases of work which are recommended for their use cannot reach the highest pinnacle of success in their service. Practically every phase of church work may be reduced to a science, humanly speaking, and like all other sciences each particular phase requires individual specific study.

(1) *The books to be used*

The right sort of textbooks must be studied. The textbooks used in the training of church members must be written by people who know their subjects through actual experience.

"Books follow sciences and not sciences books." No one can accurately set forth any phase of Christian training who has not proved by actual experience that he is master of his subject. The textbooks on any and all phases of church work should set out accurately the facts and truths involved in the subjects which they treat. The methods proposed must have been proved in experience, else the books are worthless and should find no place in the library of Christian workers.

For example, textbooks on soul-winning should be written by real soul-winners, men and women who are actually at the business of leading lost souls to know Christ as a personal Saviour.

Textbooks dealing with the art of teaching the Bible in the Sunday school should be written by men and women who are successful Sunday school teachers.

Textbooks written on Sunday school administration for use by pastors, superintendents, and other Sunday school officers must be written by those who have succeeded in the science of Sunday school building.

Provision has been made by Southern Baptists for the all-round development and training of our people. The various courses of study offer many textbooks and cover a wide range of subjects. There are courses which offer training in Sunday school methods, in Training Union work, in missions, in church music, in library work, in Baptist Student Union work, in church architecture, in visual aids.

In the Sunday School Training Course, and in the Training Union Study Courses much emphasis is given to books on the Bible, Baptist doctrine and evangelism. The study of such books should be promoted as an all-church effort. Individuals who meet the requirements may receive credit for these books in either the Sunday school or the Training Union course.

In these courses we have books dealing with various phases of Baptist church life and adapted to the needs of all Baptist church members from the boys and girls of nine years of age to the oldest and most learned. There are also books on administration, teaching and leadership designed for workers and prospective workers. The books are simple and practical in treatment, modest in price, and should be in the libraries of all pastors, deacons, Sunday school workers, and Baptist Training Union workers.

Lists of books offered in the Sunday School Training Course and information about their use may be secured from the Sunday School Department, Baptist Sunday School Board, Nashville 3, Tennessee. Pamphlets on the Training Union Study Course may be secured from the Training Union Department. Both lists may be secured from state headquarters.

(2) *Effective ways of taking these courses*

There are a number of highly effective ways of taking these training courses that every church may use. The one used most widely is the special week of training.

This method contemplates a special week of intensive training work at least four times each year, about one week each quarter. These four weeks should be marked up on the church calendar at the beginning of the year. The work usually runs from Monday to Friday, inclusive.

The books should be ordered, the teachers secured, and the enrolment of the pupils begun well in advance. In the larger churches a number of classes in different books will run simultaneously; in small churches, perhaps only one or two. This method of training Sunday school workers can be used effectively in all churches.

Suggested schedules for each night:

7:00-7:45 Class Period
7:45-8:15 Inspirational Period
8:15-9:00 Class Period

or

7:00-8:30 Class Period
8:30-9:00 Inspirational Period

Provision may be made to serve a meal prior to the first class period. The schedule will be adjusted to the needs of the particular situation. A minimum of ten forty-five-minute class periods, or the equivalent, is required.

Other plans for training Sunday school officers and teachers have also proved successful. A class may meet for one evening each week for five weeks. Special morning or afternoon classes for workers in the Extension department, and in the Cradle Roll, Beginner, and Primary groups may prove practical. The work may be carried on by individual study. (See instructions on p. 10 of this book.)

The churches can train their workers in the principles of good Sunday school work if they desire to do so. There is no doubt about it. The courses are prepared, the books are priced within the reach of all. Teachers are available for doing the work if pastors and Sunday school superintendents will only get at the business in dead earnest.

2. *Practical Laboratory Methods*

"Learning to do by doing" is a trite saying. It is also an over-towering truth. Doing and knowing go hand in hand.

(1) *Commanded in the Scriptures*

The principle that knowing must lead to doing has its foundation in the Scriptures. "If any man will do his will, he shall know of the doctrine, whether it be of God, or whether I speak of myself" (John 7:17).

"But be ye doers of the word, and not hearers only, deceiving your own selves. For if any be a hearer of the word, and not a doer, he is like unto a man beholding his natural face in a glass: for he beholdeth himself, and goeth his way, and straightway forgetteth what manner of man he was" (James 1:22-24).

(2) *Proved by experience*

No one is ever the master of any subject until he has actually given a practical demonstration of how to use the facts or truths contained in the subject.

Some one asked a skilled skater how he learned to skate. He said, "By getting up every time I fell down."

Ask the expert swimmer where he learned to swim. He will reply, "In the water."

Ask the skilled musician where he learned to play so well. He will answer, "At the piano."

Ask the successful soul-winner how he learned to win souls. He will answer, "At the business day by day."

Ask the successful Sunday school teacher the secret of his success and where he got his best training. He will answer, "In the classroom."

(3) *Needed in the Sunday school*

Under no circumstances would we underestimate the value of the theory of Sunday school training. On the contrary, as we have already stated all who undertake to work in any capacity in the Sunday school need this type of training, and they are, as a rule, effective and useful in their work in proportion to the amount of training they take. However, all the diplomas and seals and degrees in the world will no more make an effective Sunday school worker than will a college diploma, with the accompanying degrees, make a useful, successful citizen.

Sunday school workers in addition to their theoretical training must allow themselves to be put into actual service in the Sunday school and get at the business and stay at it constantly. In fact theory cannot be truly learned apart from practice.

Recently, a man died in New York City who had attended Columbia University for fifty years. He had been awarded all the degrees the University had and a number of awards were especially created for him. The last degree given him was the degree of "D.P.M.," "Doctor of Perpetual Motion." When he was a young man in college a wealthy uncle died and left him $2,500 a year as long as he attended school. All his degrees and awards were empty things. He was not an educated man nor a useful citizen because he failed to put himself in contact with humanity and work out in his life the knowledge gained in college. Individuals who pursue the training course, earning award after award, without going to work in the Sunday school are just as useless.

The other side of this matter is illustrated by the experience of an Oklahoma Indian farmer who enlisted in service for World War I and was sent to Fort Sill for training. After some months in the training camp it was found that he was absent at roll call one morning. An officer was sent in search and found him on his farm plowing. The officer tried to impress upon him the enormity of the crime of deserting the

United States Army and asked him why he had done such a thing. The Indian replied, "Too much salute, and not enough shoot."

All Sunday school workers need training in the manual of arms. They also need target practice with the enemy in sight.

(4) *Provided in the regular weekly officers and teachers' meeting*

It is doubtful if any Sunday school force of officers and teachers is 50 per cent efficient without a regular weekly meeting which provides among other things especially for a study of how to teach the Sunday school lessons for the following Sunday.

This meeting will generate and keep alive a spirit of fellowship and enthusiasm which every Sunday school must have if it does its best work, and which cannot have without such a meeting.

This meeting enables the workers to consider together all the problems in the school and reach an agreement as to their solution.

It enables the pastor to study the Sunday school organization as a whole and the officers and teachers individually, thus learning their needs, and how to sympathize with them in all their work.

It affords the officers opportunities to diagnose properly the whole Sunday school situation, locate the weakness in each department and class, and put in motion ways and means for correcting and strengthening these weak places.

It affords the inexperienced and untrained teachers opportunities for securing the help they need in methods of lesson preparation and teaching which they cannot get from any other source.

It affords the experienced and capable teachers opportunities for helping their fellow teachers both by precept and example.

Trying to conduct a successful Sunday school with a monthly workers' council in lieu of a weekly officers and teachers' meeting is like fishing in the Mississippi River with a bent pin for a hook, or hunting big game in Africa with a .22 caliber pistol.

(5) *Skill acquired through doing the work*

The true science of Sunday school building, in the last analysis, is demonstrated outside the church building in contact with people in their homes and places of business. Out there is the arena in which Sunday school warriors do their fighting.

A real Bible-teaching Sunday school is not a stage for the exhibition of church members who are prominent in business and social circles. On the contrary, it is an arena in which great contests are put on, and battles fought with the forces of evil contending for the lives and souls of lost people, and often for the lives of Christian people out of the line of duty.

A Sunday school teacher or pupil can learn more about Sunday school visiting in one hour of directed visitation in the interest of new members and absentees than he can learn from studying all the things ever written on the subject and never going out.

A Sunday school superintendent can learn more about Sunday school building by enlisting a teacher and putting into his hands a list of prospective pupils and occasionally spending an hour with this teacher in visiting these prospects than he can learn from a study of all the things ever written on the subject apart from practice.

Sunday school officers and teachers can learn more about winning lost people to Christ by taking a list of the lost people in the classes and spending one hour some afternoon or evening in visiting them in their homes, speaking a word of sympathy, praying with and seeking to win them to Christ than they can learn from a passive study of all the books written on soul-winning.

A Sunday school secretary or fieldworker can most effectively learn the science of Sunday school building by putting on some eight-day enlargement campaigns in the churches. Let him lead in taking a census of the community, grading and tabulating the results, and enlarging the Sunday school organization to reach all the prospective pupils found. Let him direct the workers in visiting all these prospects, inviting them to attend the Sunday school, reorganizing, grading, and reclassifying the school and putting in the Six Point Record System. He will learn more from such experience than from studying all the books written on Sunday school administration, and attending training schools for a lifetime, and never trying to put the theories into practice.

It is important, however, to keep the theory and practice in proper balance. We "learn by doing" provided the doing is directed according to right principles. The practical efforts at visitation, at enlistment, at soul-winning, at Sunday school building must all be evaluated according to approved methods. Thus errors will be pointed out, difficulties cleared up, and improvements suggested. This will prepare the worker to try again and to profit by his doing.

The recent trend in training is toward Sunday school clinics, emphasizing administration or and Bible teaching. These are designed to combine directed practice with the study of theory, and interrelate the two. If our people—pastors, superintendents, and other workers—are ever to learn the real science of Sunday school work they must learn it in the laboratory of actual experience, guided by the theory which has already proved effective.

Section V of the workbook will help class members to summarize some main points in this chapter.

CHAPTER VI

THE SUNDAY SCHOOL FUNCTIONING IN THE SERVICE OF WORSHIP

The object of this study is to show how the Sunday school organization may be made to contribute in a great way to practically every phase of the church's work, and by so doing add to the efficiency and power of the Sunday school as an effective Bible teaching agency.

We have seen that Bible study must lead to participation in all phases of the work of the church. One of the most important functions of the Sunday school is to bring into the preaching service on Sunday morning all those who attend Sunday school.

All the workers need to understand that the work of the Sunday school is not completed at the close of the teaching session. The Sunday school in a body should attend the eleven o'clock service of worship, and the pastor and the other officers and teachers should realize that it is incumbent upon them to see that this is done.

In order to get this matter before us in a simple, practical way, we wish to ask and answer three questions, as follows:

Why should there be a large congregation at every preaching service?

What effect does the faithful proclamation of the gospel usually produce in the lives of those who attend the preaching service regularly?

How may the Sunday school organization be used in securing the regular attendance of the pupils upon the services of worship?

Let us study each of these questions closely.

I. WHY SHOULD THERE BE A LARGE CONGREGATION AT EVERY PREACHING SERVICE?

The New Testament exhorts us, "Let us consider one another to provoke unto love and to good works: not forsaking the assembling of ourselves together. . ." (Heb. 10:24-25).

Common sense would indicate the wisdom of using the Sunday school to lead people to obey this command.

1. *To Make Use of the House of Worship*

In every situation the house of worship should be used. Auditorium space is provided at large expense and is used for the formal preaching of the gospel only four or five days in each month—104 times each year. It is, therefore, of great importance that every available seat should be provided with an occupant every time the church house is open for worship.

In the rural sections where churches have preaching only one Sunday in each month—certainly, every available seat should be filled. On the Sundays the pastor is not there, the Sunday school will provide a worship service at the regular preaching hour, and certainly the house should be filled then also.

Each of these church houses represents a comparatively large financial investment, and from a standpoint of common sense and economy each and every one of them should be used as often as possible and should be filled with people at every service.

2. *It Is the Pastor's Best Opportunity to Reach the Multitudes with the Gospel*

During the earthly ministry of Jesus and the apostles and for many years following, there were no church houses as we have them today. There were no beautiful auditoriums in those days with splended organs, highly trained chorus choirs and comfortable seats. Occasionally Jesus and the apostles preached in the Jewish synagogues, but for the greater part they chose to preach wherever they drew a crowd together—on the streets, by the riverside, by the seaside, on the highways, in the homes of the people.

How different it is today in this land of ours where houses of worship abound everywhere! There is comparatively little preaching on the streets or in open-air meetings. Houses of worship have been built and are being built easily accessible to nearly everybody. Especially is this true in the South.

People must attend the houses of worship if they are to hear the message. The opportunity the preacher has to proclaim the gospel of life and peace is largely restricted to the congregation in the house of worship. If the people do not attend, in that proportion is the preacher's opportunity lost, and the gospel message made to fail because of the lack of hearers. Therefore, every house of worship should be filled to overflowing every time the gospel is proclaimed.

3. *All People Need to Hear the Gospel Message Proclaimed*

Attendance upon Sunday school Sunday morning, no matter how good the school may be, is not sufficient to supply the spiritual needs of the people. To be sure, they need the Sunday school. They also need the preaching service. They need the Sunday school plus the preaching service. It is not only a prerogative of the officers and teachers to see that all pupils attend the services of worship; it is their imperative duty to do this.

In our city churches sometimes the Sunday school attendance is even larger than the preaching congregation, and for the most part of an entirely different personnel. This state of affairs should not be tolerated for one moment by the pastor, the superintendent, and the teachers.

The main instrument to be used in winning lost people to Christ and building them up in the most holy faith is the preaching of the gospel, and it is the duty of the officers and teachers of the Sunday School to bring their pupils under its influence whenever and wherever an opportunity is offered.

II. What Will Be the Effects of the Faithful Proclamation of the Gospel?

In the sight of God, people are divided into two classes, those who are lost and those who are saved. Both these classes need the preaching service.

1. *The Lost Will Be Won to Christ*

It is doubtful if we properly estimate the condition of people who have not taken Christ as their Saviour. We speak calmly about them as being "unsaved." Is this a proper designation for the condition of one who is far away from God, wandering in sin, without God, and without hope in the world? Such a person is lost, with all that the word means and is unable to find his way.

The Bible describes such a person as being "dead in trespasses and in sin." Anew and afresh we need to get it upon our hearts that the members of our households, our friends, the multitudes of men and women and boys and girls all around us who have not accepted Christ as their Saviour are dead, and that they need to be brought into contact with the life-giving stream of the gospel of Christ which alone brings life.

The public proclamation of the gospel by the preacher has a distinctive and large place in bringing lost people to Christ. Let us see particularly some of the results of the right sort of preaching in the lives of people who are lost.

(1) It produces conviction for sin.
(2) It brings to repentance.
(3) It brings to confession of Jesus as Saviour.

Sunday after Sunday as pupils who do not know Christ sit quietly in the congregation listening to the proclamation of the gospel of life, the Holy Spirit has an opportunity to work upon their hearts and consciences and use the preached word to convict them of sin. On occasion like this and in an atmosphere like this it is comparatively easy for lost people to choose Jesus and make a public profession of their faith in him.

Great is the Sunday school teacher's privilege to sow the life-giving seed of the gospel in the hearts of lost pupils and water it with his tears. But it is the preacher's incomparable opportunity to bring individuals to repentance and confession in the services of public worship.

A church which does not use its Sunday school to get numbers of lost people into the preaching services is asleep and sinfully derelict in its duty.

2. *The Saved Will Be Built Up in the Faith*

The place and power of the preached Word in the life of the Christian is regarded all too lightly even by many experienced Christians. Attendance upon the services of worship is often made a matter of convenience rather than regarded as a great privilege and sacred duty. It is often regulated by the state of the weather, one's feelings, one's admiration, or lack of admiration, for the preacher.

Public worship is an absolute essential in the life of a Christian, and he suffers irreparable loss every time he allows anything but providential hindrance to prevent his attendance upon these services.

Let us see what regular attendance upon the preaching services does for those who love Christ:

(1) Guards against temptations.
(2) Corrects conduct.
(3) Throws light on the problems of life.
(4) Increases spiritual growth.
(5) Brings hope to the discouraged and downhearted.
(6) Brings a determination to serve Christ.

It is presumed of course that the preaching will be of the right kind, the Bible kind, the kind of preaching that the Apostles Peter, James, John, and Paul did, the kind that Philip, Stephen, and Timothy did. One has only to study the Bible account of their sermons to be convinced that they did not make an effort to give exhibitions of their scholarship.

They did not try to please a few eminent church members, judges, lawyers, professors, and rich people. Their preaching was in the "demonstration and power

of the Holy Spirit." Their preaching honored the
Word of God and exalted Christ. Their preaching
brought conviction and confession and turning away
from sin. Their preaching resulted in godliness of life
on the part of Christians and a determination to live
like Christ and serve him only.

In no sense is it to be understood that individual
work for individuals is to be discounted. It is of the
utmost importance, and the only method by which multitudes of Christians will ever win the lost to Christ.
However, along with this method of personal work, we
are emphasizing the need of the pastor's having a multitude of people in his congregation every time he
stands to preach the gospel.

Any pastor or any Sunday school superintendent who
can stand at the door of the church house Sunday morning between the Sunday school session and the service
of worship and watch unmoved as Sunday school pupils
swarm out into the streets and rapidly disappear, needs
to be shocked and dislodged from an attitude of com-
placency concerning this all-important matter.

Any preacher anywhere can preach to practically
his entire Sunday school every Sunday morning if he
earnestly desires to do so, and will pursue the practical
methods suggested.

III. How Can Attendance of Sunday School Pupils
     at the Services of Worship Be Secured?

The pastor and the Sunday school superintendent
should have a "heart's desire" that pupils should attend the morning preaching service. This is much more
than a wish. It is a desire backed by a knowledge of
what regular attendance upon the preaching services
will mean in the lives of individuals.

Practically all pupils can be induced to attend the regular morning service of worship if the proper means are employed. Finding fault here as everywhere else is futile. Something constructive must be done. Some suggestions are submitted which, when properly carried out, will prove efficacious under all conditions.

1. *Use the Unified Service*

The unified service means that the Sunday school session and the eleven o'clock service of public worship are combined. The Sunday school by departments and classes above the Primary age group, is brought together into the main auditorium on Sunday morning at the close of the lesson or department period. Beginner and Primary pupils are turned over to their parents or other members of the family. Younger children should be cared for in the Nurseries.

At a given signal each department, headed by the department superintendent and accompanied by the other department officers and teachers, should march in a body into the main auditorium and be conducted by the church ushers to the place which has been assigned to it. In a class Sunday school, members will come in by classes. The pastor and the general superintendent should be on the platform as they march in and accord them a smiling welcome.

In a well-arranged building a Sunday school of 2,500 members may be brought into the auditorium and seated in five minutes' time if the proceding is characterized by order and system.

After the Sunday school is seated, an interesting and helpful period of song and prayer should be presented, followed by reports. The whole should not last more than fifteen minutes. The superintendent may lead in this part of the service, and the pastor should always participate with appropriate words and go into the service of public worship without a break.

See chapter 7 of *Building a Standard Sunday School,* for a fuller discussion of the Unified Service.

2. *Use the Six Point Record System*

Where this system of Sunday school bookkeeping is correctly operated, every Sunday morning each member is reminded as he makes his report for the day that he is expected to remain for the service of public worship. His grade is affected by his attitude toward the preaching service. The majority of Sunday school members will not long remain indifferent regarding attendance at preaching service when brought face to face with the matter regularly each week as they mark their records.

The record regarding preaching attendance will reveal individual needs to teachers and class officers, and form the basis for visitation. It will point to the need for teaching the value of public worship in the classrooms and the assembly programs.

For a fuller discussion see *The Six Point Record System and Its Use* by Noland and the free literature on the subject issued by the Baptist Sunday School Board.

3. *Use the Weekly Officers and Teachers' Meetings*

A week-by-week study of the records in the weekly officers and teachers' meetings will reveal the number of people who leave Sunday school without attending the morning preaching service. It will show which classes need to put forth particular effort at this point. It will direct teachers to the study of individual records to determine which members need help in forming the habit of preaching attendance.

In the workers' meetings training can be given in how to visit to promote preaching attendance. Too often visitation is limited to efforts to win new members and bring back absentees. The visitation ministry should be enlarged to include personal work with individuals who need encouragement in forming any of the habits involved in the Six Point Record System. It should include loving, Spirit-led contacts to help with any spiritual need in the life of any member.

4. *Use the Teaching Opportunities in Assembly and Class Periods*

The assembly programs and the class periods on Sunday morning offer opportunities to teach the value of attending the public worship services. In the weekly officers and teachers' meeting, plan assembly programs based on this objective. Help teachers to plan lesson procedures which shall lead class members to conviction regarding the value of attendance at the preaching service, and to change of conduct in this vital matter.

If officers and teachers will get on their hearts a deep concern to see every member of the Sunday school attend the preaching service unless providentially hindered, and if they will plan administration and teaching procedures to promote this objective, they can use the Sunday school to put lost people and saved people into the public worship service every Sunday morning.

Turn to Section VI of the workbook in the appendix and use a few minutes in the class period to follow the directions given there, and then to discuss the answers together.

CHAPTER VII

THE SUNDAY SCHOOL FUNCTIONING AS A SOUL-WINNING AGENCY

According to figures compiled by the Department of Survey, Statistics, and Information, every year hundreds of churches in the Southern Baptist Convention do not report a single baptism.

It is serious for even one church, to say nothing of hundreds, to be in such a condition. One wonders what these churches and their pastors were doing.

It is probable that some of these churches were pastorless. However, being without a pastor could not absolve a church of the Lord Jesus from blame for not attending to the main business committed to it by the great Head of the churches.

It would seem that any church that goes through an entire year without winning at least one sinner to Christ, certainly does not manifest the mind and spirit of Christ. No doubt in all of these churches some of the members cherished a soul-winning desire. But the churches lacked a definite, purposeful evangelistic program, and so the year closed without a harvest of souls.

Every church of the Lord Jesus should take account of its resources and possibilities for winning to Christ lost people near its doors. Each year it should plan an adequate program for doing the work dearest to the heart of Christ.

I. An Adequate Soul-Winning Program

What should constitute an adequate program of evangelism for a Baptist church?

1. *Special Periods Are Inadequate*

Seasons of special effort to win the lost, with the pastor or an invited evangelist doing the preaching, are most desirable, but of themselves they are not adequate to meet the soul needs of all the lost people of any community. On these occasions many will accept Christ, but a large number will not. These seasons of special evangelistic effort should be only a part of a church's program for winning the lost to Christ.

"Decision Days" in the Sunday school from time to time do not constitute an adequate soul-winning program. The fact is, this is a method fraught with grave danger, and if used at all should be led by the pastor, and he should be sure that he is following the leadership of the Holy Spirit. At best this method is only partial, and even when combined with the annual protracted meeting it is not sufficient as a soul-winning program of a church.

There are churches that concentrate their efforts to win the lost in a so-called "soul-winning drive" which culminates in a "decision day" and baptizing on "Easter Sunday." This custom is not only without scriptural warrant, but anti-Biblical. Any church which pursues this custom may expect to find its members destitute of a passion for the souls of men and lacking in conviction that people without Christ are eternally lost.

When a church confines its soul-winning operations to special days and annual protracted meetings, it does violence to the souls of lost people, quenches the soul-winning spirit of the members of the churches and

limits God's power to save to certain times and occasions, and thus fails to function properly as a divine
lighthouse.

2. Complete Enlistment Sought

It is heartening indeed to realize that in all the
churches there are faithful Christians who keep the
soul-winning fires burning in their own hearts. The
pastor may always count upon the few to pray for and
seek the lost people in the community.

Usually the Sunday school officers and teachers are
in this number. But this is not sufficient. The "faithful
few" should be multiplied many times over until every
church will have instead the "faithful many," upon
whom the pastor may rely to search for the lost until
they find them and bring them to Christ.

3. Constant Efforts Essential

New Testament evangelism was continuous. "And
the Lord added unto them day by day those who were
being saved" (Acts 2:47 RSV). The early Christians
did not employ spasmodic efforts for teaching and
preaching to lost people. They did not set aside a stated
or special week each year in which to win lost people
to Christ. They believed that those who had not accepted Christ as Saviour were lost every week and
every day in the year, and they went after them for
Christ continuously.

When they were saved they were baptized immediately. They were not put on probation or saved up
for a gala occasion in the spring as is the custom of
some churches now.

An adequate soul-winning program for a church
must take into consideration that people who have not
accepted Christ are lost—lost now and eternally! The

sinner's only salvation is today—"Now is the accepted time; behold now is the day of salvation" (2 Cor. 6:2).

4. A Church Program Needed

What are churches for, anyway? Are they not to carry out the will and complete the work of Christ in the world? Jesus said of himself and to us, "As my Father hath sent me, even so send I you" (John 20:21). Again, "For the Son of man is come to seek and to save that which was lost" (Luke 19:10). And again, "I am come that they might have life, and that they might have it more abundantly" (John 10:10). Also the apostle Paul said of him, "Christ Jesus came into the world to save sinners" (1 Tim. 1:15).

The soul-wining program of a church should be comprehensive enough to permit and encourage every member of the church and every organization in the church to participate. It should be so wide in its scope, so comprehensive in its plans, so constant in its efforts and so dead in earnest in its endeavor that people everywhere will be impressed with the fact that the church's chief business is to win the lost to a saving knowledge of Christ.

5. Pastoral Leadership Determines Results

The pastor is the watchman of the tower—the watcher for souls. He is God's man to lead his church, every member of it, after souls. If the pastor does not do it, it will not be done.

No church will go ahead of its pastor in doing this divine task. If the pastor is without passion for the souls of men and if he does not have a program which takes into account all the lost people in the community near at hand as well as those far away, his church will not have such a vision. There can be no doubt that the pastor's chief business is to lead in this, the chief business of the church.

In this connection L. R. Scarborough in *With Christ After the Lost* says:

"The first preachers Christ called in his earthly ministry met the words 'Follow me and I will make you fishers of men' falling from Christ's lip, as their first ordination task. The last command of the ascending Saviour was 'Go ye . . . and make disciples of all nations.' Between the holy call and the last commission Christ put the primary and ever-present duty of his preachers to be winners of souls. Whatever else he calls them to, he does not call them from this high duty. To this one end Christ came to seek and to save the lost, and to this unchanging work Paul always pressed, 'I am become all things to all men that by all means I might save some.' Christ says, 'As the Father sent me, so also I send you.' and his task was ever to seek and to save that which was lost."

II. THE CHURCH'S SOUL-WINNING PROGRAM MADE PRACTICAL IN THE SUNDAY SCHOOL

Evangelism is not a plus added to the regular program; it is the main work of the Sunday school and must be interwoven in all the activities of all the departments.

1. *The Pastor and General Superintendent Leading*

A soul-winning Sunday school will not come into being nor continue to exist apart from the aggressive leadership of the pastor and superintendent.

(1) *In purpose*

Perhaps the best thing any preacher can do is to imbue his Sunday school superintendent with the purpose and spirit of the soul-winner. The pastor and superintendent must purpose in their hearts that the men and women in the Young People's and Adult classes, as well as the boys and girls in the Junior and Intermediate age groups, shall be won to Christ. They will materialize a soul-winning program, and rest neither day nor night until it is carried to a glorious consummation.

(2) *In prayer*

Whenever a pastor and Sunday school superintendent blend their prayers unceasingly for the salvation of lost people, in that place is found the Spirit of God at work on the consciences of lost people. There one will find a spirit of soul-winning fervor on the part of the people.

A few brief months of joyous experience with Allen Fort (of hallowed memory) helped the author to realize the power of a praying preacher with the soul-winning passion. Never were we together that Dr. Fort did not suggest that we pray if the place were at all suitable. Always the main burden of the prayer was in behalf of the lost people in the Sunday school and community.

No wonder that fifty-seven men and women and boys and girls from the Sunday school found Christ at the regular eleven o'clock preaching services during the last four months of his life. He literally fulfilled the Bible injunction to "pray without ceasing." A praying pastor and a praying superintendent are irresistible in attacking the stronghold of Satan at any and every point. Soon they will develop a band of praying officers and teachers.

(3) *In plans*

An effective soul-winning program must have intelligent, prayerful, painstaking planning back of it. Nothing may be left to chance. The pastor and superintendent should plan this phase of work thoroughly.

The superintendent should see that all teachers are provided with a correct list of names of the lost pupils in their classes, that they attend the weekly officers and teachers' meeting regularly, that frequently at the close of the meeting they publicly express an interest in the salvation of these pupils, and solicit the prayers of all the officers and teachers in their behalf.

At times teachers may be asked to report the number of unconverted in their classes; also, the number who have made profession of faith in Christ during a given period. In the event that there are officers and teachers in the Sunday school who are indifferent to the salvation of the lost, a procedure of this kind should help them to warm their hearts anew with a genuine soul-winning fervor.

Five or ten minutes during the administrative period at each officers and teachers' meeting would be sufficient for this. The information thus gained would furnish the pastor and the superintendent with valuable suggestions for their personal work program. It would also indicate to them the departments or classes they should visit for the purpose of making a definite appeal to the pupils to accept Christ.

(4) *In performance*

The pastor and the superintendent must set the example in carrying out a well-defined purpose and program of winning the lost to Christ. Jesus said, "My Father worketh hitherto, and I work" (John 5: 17). "I must work the works of him that sent me, while it is day: the night cometh, when no man can work" (John 9:4).

The Holy Spirit is at work in the hearts and upon the consciences of sinners. Many of them, yea, multitudes of them, are ready to accept Christ if they only knew how. But a human soul-winner is needed to co-operate with the Holy Spirit, and point them to the "Lamb of God that taketh away the sin of the world." The Holy Spirit showed the jailer how he was a lost sinner, and Paul and Silas told him how to be saved.

The soul-winning business requires action on the part of men, red hot with the soul-winning glow.

> Time worketh, let me work, too;
> Time undoeth, let me do;
> As busy as time, my work I'll ply
> Till I rest in the rest of eternity.
>
> Sin worketh, let me work, too;
> Sin undoeth, let me do;
> As busy as sin, my work I'll ply,
> Till I rest in the rest of eternity.
>
> Death worketh, let me work, too;
> Death undoeth, let me do;
> As busy as death, my work I'll ply,
> Till I rest in the rest of eternity.
>
> —Horatius Bonar

2. *The Department Superintendents Co-operating*

Without the wholehearted co-operation and leadership of each department superintendent there can be but little doing. He must swing his department into line in this program of winning the lost. There can be no time wasted here. Besides the lost boys and girls, there are grown young people and mature men and women to be won.

The superintendent should have a list showing the names of the lost people in his department by classes. He will form a holy alliance with the pastor and general superintendent, teachers, and class officers in their behalf.

The Cradle Roll and Extension departments will make lists by districts. Workers with the younger age groups will give special attention to lost parents.

Certainly there should be definite seasons of prayer for the lost pupils above Primary age. Oft-repeated opportunities should be given in the departments for them to confess Christ. These special evangelistic appeals in the assembly programs and class periods require prayerful, intelligent co-operation of the department and class organizations, working in harmony with the general superintendent and pastor. Usually the pastor is the one to make the appeal, but at times the superintendents and teachers may do so.

These special efforts may prove very effective. It is often easier for the lost to take the first step in the department or class. However, all who accept Christ should be urged to make a public profession immediately before the entire congregation at the preaching hour, and to follow Christ in baptism and church membership.

3. *The Teachers Majoring on Soul-Winning*

In this work lies the teacher's best opportunity to make his life tell for Jesus. He should have a complete prayer list of all the lost pupils in his class and daily spread this list out before God and claim his promise to save them. Each one by name should be presented at the throne of grace.

The teacher of pupils above Primary age should always be ready to make application of the lesson to those who are saved and to those in the class who are not Christians.

The teacher will do well to fall back on Isaiah 55. He may wish to memorize the entire chapter. When impatient or discouraged he should feed his soul on verses 10 and 11, then teach and plead for a verdict each and every time he comes before the class.

A praying, interested teacher can keep the soul-winning fires burning in the class. At every meeting of officers of a Young People's or an Adult class, the class officers and the teacher should bring the matter of the salvation of the lost members of the class before the group. Special prayers should be offered in their behalf and definite plans matured, looking toward their salvation.

If there are no unsaved enrolled in the class, it should be a matter of deep concern. Lost people are all around our churches, and no class should be satisfied unless it is reaching them.

4. Special Appeals Made in the Programs and Class Periods

This is a matter requiring the intelligent co-operation of the department and class organizations, working in harmony with the general superintendent and pastor. Usually the pastor is the one to make these appeals, but at times the department superintendents and teachers may do so. Special appeals in the departments or classes are very effective. It is often easier for the lost to take the first step in the department or class. However, all who accept Christ should be urged to make public profession immediately before the entire congregation at the preaching hour, join the church, and be baptized.

5. Preaching Attendance of Lost People the Responsibility of Sunday School Workers

The entire Sunday school, from the Junior department up, should attend the morning preaching service. They may come in a body, that is, by age-groups. This is the teacher's opportunity to make his teaching effective by bringing his pupils into the preaching service. This is the pastor's opportunity to reinforce the teaching process by the preaching process and call lost pupils to come to Christ.

All the Sunday school administration should magnify the importance of the preaching service. The Record System promotes it. Teachers and officers should exert their influence in the matter. Visits should be made for personal work with individuals who do not habitually remain for the preaching service.

6. *Special Seasons of Training in Soul-Winning Effective*

The best way to train soul-winners is to give them a course in soul-winning, and, at the same time, lead them in the work of actually winning souls. Each year pastors should conduct one or more classes in the science of personal evangelism. There are a number of suitable books from which to select. The following are suggested:

> *How to Win to Christ*—Burroughs
> *Soul-Winning Doctrines*—Turner
> *The Way Made Plain*—Brookes
> *The Place of the Sunday School in Evangelism*—
>   Barnette

Credit on these books is given in either the Training Union Study Course or the Sunday School Training Course. Sunday school credits are available for individuals fifteen years of age or older. Intermediates may study *Witnessing for Christ*, Ethel Hudson Williams, or *Intermediate Fishers*, Frank E. Burkhalter, and receive Training Union credit.

In order to make such meetings highly resultful, several weeks for preparation should be used. The books should be ordered well in advance. All the deacons, Sunday school officers, teachers, class officers, and as many as possible of the Sunday school members who are Christians should be enlisted to take the work.

The special efforts may continue eight days from Sunday to Sunday. Four things should characterize the week's work: prayer, study, personal work, and reports.

Prayer for the lost should be made all through the week, both day and night. There should be two study periods of forty-five minutes each evening from Monday through Friday with an intermission between the class periods for prayer. At this time assignments should be made of names of the unconverted in the Sunday school and others in the community who are known to be lost. Only one or two names should be assigned to each worker, who should agree that before attending the meeting the following evening he will pray for each one thus assigned to him, and will, if possible, speak a personal word about Christ to each one.

Often personal workers will be able to bring to the meeting with them those whom they have won to Christ during the day. When reports are called for, the latter may be given an opportunity to make a public profession of faith in Christ.

On the Sunday preceding this special effort of training and winning, the pastor may wish to preach a sermon on prayer and one on personal work. The Sunday following he may feel led to direct both sermons to lost people, and to give the invitation for them to accept Christ and join the church.

Section VII of the workbook in the appendix will furnish a basis for summarizing this chapter.

CHAPTER VIII

THE SUNDAY SCHOOL FUNCTIONING AS A CHURCH FINANCING AGENCY

In his book, *Our Lord and Ours,* Dr. P. E. Burroughs truly and pointedly says, "The very life and progress of a church depends upon sound financing." Churches which habitually remain in arrears for running expenses and missions are usually destitute of attractiveness and charm; they drag along at a poor dying rate, and for the most part are purposeless, passionless, and powerless.

It is not a sin for a church to be in debt for some things. Under proper circumstances a church may owe a balance on its building which has been erected for the purpose of doing better work, or it may owe for some necessary items of equipment such as an organ, pianos, or pews, and at the same time maintain its self-respect, the respect of the community, and a high state of spiritual power. However, it is reprehensible and shameful for a church of the Lord Jesus Christ to keep continually in arrears for running expenses and its missionary program.

I. Some Causes Why Churches Are in Arrears for Running Expenses and Missions

The great majority of churches which find themselves confronted with a deficit for current expenses and missions are in this deplorable condition not because of necessity, but for lack of executive leadership in planning and operating their financial affairs. The pastors, deacons, and finance committees are not informed as to the most effective method of church financing, or they are careless and slack concerning their church's financial standing before God.

1. *No Financial Program*

Some churches live from hand-to-mouth, trusting to "luck" that something will happen to keep them afloat. The members are ever in a state of spiritual starvation. The church is always on the defensive. It wages no vigorous warfare against sin at home and does almost nothing toward sending the gospel to the uttermost parts of the earth, because it does not have any financial program at all.

2. *An Inadequate Financial Program*

The plans of some churches are partial. They include only a few of the objects fostered by their denomination and a very small minority of the members participate with any degree of regularity. Their efforts are characterized by spasms rather than system. The members are prodded from time to time by the pastor and finance committee. They are urged to "give until it hurts." Under such conditions it "hurts" to give anything. Such churches are in a constant state of pain, and go along year after year like a man on crutches.

3. *An Unworked Program*

Others leave their plan to run itself and before the year is half gone they find themselves in arrears on running expenses and missions. Two or three high-powered special collections are put in during the year. At the close of the year, if a deficit is faced another special offering is called for, or the deacons go to the bank and borrow the money hoping in "same way to pull out" during the ensuing year.

In order for a church to keep out of debt for running expenses and missions, properly maintain itself and be free to conduct a vigorous offensive, it must have a sound financial system which functions fifty-two weeks in the year.

II. What a Sound Financial Program Will Accomplish

We may not agree as to details in the financial program for a Baptist church, but certainly we are agreed that an adequate system should accomplish two things: It should educate and enlist in scriptural giving every man, woman, and child who regularly attends the service of the church. It should keep the church free from debt for current expenses and missions. Let us take up these two items and examine them briefly in detail.

1. *Educate and Enlist in Scriptural Giving*

Church members and nonchurch members alike who attend the Sunday school and Baptist Training Union as well as those who attend the preaching services will be educated and enlisted in scriptural giving by a sound financial system. The churches are obligated to educate and enlist in the grace of giving all who participate in any of the activities and all who attend any of the services. When a church fails to do this it robs individuals of spiritual blessings which come only through faithful stewardship of their means.

Surveys reveal that sometimes even less than 50 per cent of the members are regular contributors to the church's financial program, to say nothing of the numbers of nonchurch members among the Sunday school pupils and others attending the services of worship.

It is revealing to compare the church treasurer's book and the church membership roll.

Sometime the so-called every-member canvass includes only the large givers and the more prominent men and women of the church who are easily reached. An effective program of enlistment must take into consideration the multitude of small givers, including the young people and the children, who belong to the church. Furthermore, the nonchurch members who regularly attend the services of the church, both Sunday school and preaching services, are never thought of in connection with the every-member canvass.

An adequate financial church program will include all church members and all others who regularly attend any of the services of the church.

2. *Keep the Churches Free from Debt*

In practically all Baptist churches sufficient funds are accessible and may be made available to defray all local expenses and make regular worthy contributions to all denominational causes. The great need is a sound, adequate financial system correctly operated.

When the churches in the Southern Baptist Convention adopt and operate a sound financial program, how will it affect the Lord's work?

Practically every church in the Southern Baptist Convention now receiving aid from its State Mission Board would become self-supporting and a regular contributor to the denominational program.

Our boards and educational institutions would have the finances needed for advance.

At the end of the first twelve months the Southern Baptist Convention would be able to double its missionary forces on all its mission fields both at home and in foreign lands.

Practically every church now maintaining a half-time or fourth-time pastorate would be able to support a pastor for full time at a good salary.

All pastors' salaries could be advanced to a point to give every preacher a comfortable living and a comfortable house in which to live.

All the churches now needing buildings would be able to build or remodel to provide houses adapted for carrying out an adequate program of preaching, teaching, and training.

Our state mission boards would be able to assist in the organization and maintainance of churches and in the erection of church houses on every hill and in every valley where churches are needed in the entire territory of the Southern Baptist Convention.

In the last analysis then, it behooves us to use the scriptural system of church financing and get all the churches to adopt and correctly operate this system. For only when this is done, will Southern Baptists be able to launch a worthy worldwide program of conquest for Christ.

III. The Unified Budget Operated Through the Sunday School

The Unified Budget operated by the church through its Sunday school organization is confidently claimed by pastors, deacons, and church finance committees to meet the need for a sound financial policy for a church. Let us examine briefly some of the distinguishing marks of this system.

1. *Under Church Control and Direction*

The pastors, deacons, and finance committees have the oversight and direction of the inauguration and operation of the entire budget. The church determines what the budget shall include and how much shall be devoted to each of the different objects fostered by the church. All money goes into one treasury; all accounts are kept by the church treasurer.

2. *An All-Inclusive Budget*

An all-inclusive budget includes all church expenses and expenditures—all salaries, running expenses, missions, benevolences, and the expenses of all the church's activities such as the Sunday school, Baptist Training Union, Woman's Missionary Union, and every other organization, activity, agency, and cause fostered by the church.

3. *One Treasurer—the Church Treasurer*

The Unified Budget thus properly operated does away with the treasurers of the different agencies of the church such as the Sunday school, Baptist Training Union, and the Woman's Missionary Union. The church treasurer receives and disburses all the funds.

4. *One Offering—A Church Offering*

The Unified Budget thus operated does away with the multiplicity of offerings. It provides for one offering each week, and that a church offering. There are no more separate collections for Sunday school work, Baptist Training Union work, or Woman's Missionary Union. The offerings made at the meetings of these organizations go into the church treasury for the support of the entire church program.

5. *Each Member Giving Every Week*

The Unified Budget thus operated calls for a weekly offering from every one who attends any of the services of the church, nonchurch members and church members alike. This offering is made at the first service attended during the day whether the Sunday school, the morning preaching service, the Baptist Training Union or the evening preaching service. It goes to the support of the entire church program.

Thus we see that the Unified Budget is all-inclusive in deed and in truth. It includes all church expenses and expenditures, all the agencies and organizations of the church, the preaching of the gospel by the church, both at home and to the ends of the earth, and all the benevolences of the church. Likewise, it includes as a regular giver every man, woman, and child who comes under the influence of the church.

6. *A Trained, Systematic Organization to Make It Go*

No plan will succeed, no matter how good, if left to work itself. An extensive organization and much time are required even in the smallest churches to keep in personal touch with each and every one who should contribute regularly to the church's financial program.

The Sunday school organization is logically the one body through which a church has personal touch with the greater part of its entire constituency once each week. The Sunday school officers and teachers have personal knowledge of every member of the Sunday school, (which should include every member of the church) and so are in a position to lead individuals to participate in the financial program. Once they have caught the vision they can lead the Sunday school in inaugurating and successfully operating the Unified Budget.

7. *An Effective Record System*

The Unified Budget worked through the Sunday school can be made successful in the highest degree only through the proper operation of the Six Point Record System. This system acquaints the pastor, the finance committee, and the officers and teachers each week with the standing of every member of the Sunday school in his relation to the budget.

Each member can be furnished a monthly report card which shows his budget standing as well as his standing in the Six Point Record System. No one is allowed to get behind with his offerings without having his attention called to it. The small givers as well as the large givers are looked after. The children as well as their parents receive undivided attention; no one is neglected. Thus this system successfully enlists a great throng of small givers in the budget and then keeps in sympathetic touch with each of these weekly. As a means of developing the individual, it has proved its worth.

IV. The Inauguration and Operation of the Unified Budget Through the Sunday School

It is folly to set out to change the financial system of a church without giving time to prayer and a program of educating the people.

1. *Setting Up the Budget*

To begin with, there may be a small committee, elected by the church, and including the pastor, whose business it shall be to study the whole situation and recommend a weekly budget to the church for adoption. This committee should be sympathetic with all the agencies and activities of the church, and should include in the budget sufficient funds to finance all the organizations and interests of the church without embarrassment to any of them.

At the proper time this committee may be enlarged to include representatives of the various church agencies so that the needs of all will be fully considered.

In this connection, we quote from a statement by a successful pastor.

"Three months or longer before the fiscal year begins, a committee should be appointed by the church to recommend a budget. If records have been kept, the church office can furnish an itemized statement of current expenses and all contributions for the past two or three years. The Sunday school superintendent can secure a carefully prepared statement of the needs of each department. The president of the Woman's Missionary Union, the director of the Baptist Training Union, and the president of the Brotherhood will be requested to furnish the same information for their organizations. The house committee will furnish an estimate of the money needed for repairs and equipment. Other standing committees will state their needs.

"With the foregoing information in hand the budget committee can arrive at a safe estimate of the expenses for the year, always allowing for growth and expansion. The needs of the denominational program may be met by agreement that all money contributed shall be divided, say on a fifty-fifty basis, between local expenses and missions and benevolences. When the report is complete the budget will be presented to the church in conference for final approval. This report should be printed and distributed so that each member may see amounts allocated and understand every recommendation made."

2. *Informing the Members*

The highest success in this important undertaking can be reached only through a widespread informational campaign. This preparation period should cover from six weeks to two months.

At the very beginning a day should be set on which the every-member canvass is to be made. The people should be informed. This may be done through teaching, preaching, and praying.

Churchwide mission study classes promoted by the Woman's Missionary Union and the Baptist Brotherhood, stewardship classes for all the church promoted by the Baptist Training Union, sermons and prayer meeting talks by the pastor—all these help to inform the people. It is profitable to hold an all-day prayer service to which every member of the church is asked to come at least for a few minutes at some time during the day from eight o'clock in the morning until nine o'clock in the evening.

The plan for using the Sunday school as the church financing agency should be presented briefly at the weekly officers and teachers' meetings. It should be explained in assembly programs, and promoted in the classes by teachers and stewardship vice-presidents.

The Baptist Brotherhood, the Training Union, and the Woman's Missionary Union should join in the campaign to inform every member.

Publicity should include placards with appropriate Scriptures mottoes and slogans, appropriate banners in each auditorium and classroom, the budget printed in the church bulletin, letters from the pastor and finance committee to every member of the church and to all Sunday school pupils not members of the church.

3. *Inaugurating the Plan*

We have discussed the matter of publicity, the appointment and the work of the budget committee, and the adoption of the budget by the church. We now come to the work of installing the budget.

The deacons and finance committee should set the example by signing subscription cards. They are the leaders and what they do will in a large measure determine what the whole church will do. After these leaders have made their subscriptions they will then be able to get behind the proposition with the utmost earnestness and enthusiasm.

At a regular weekly meeting of the officers and teachers of the Sunday school, each officers and teacher should sign a subscription card to the budget. They are church-elected leaders of the Sunday school, and this definite action is necessary in order to put each and every one of them back of the budget with the greatest enthusiasm.

The budget chairman should ask the department superintendents each to accept a quota for his department. This should be carefully worked out ahead of time by the finance committee, the pastor, and the Sunday school superintendent. It should be thoroughly explained that this is in no wise an assessment but a suggestion of an amount for each department to subscribe, subject to change if the department superintendents so desire.

After the quotas have been accepted by each department superintendent the workers' meeting should adjourn and meet in department groups. Here each class in the Young People's and Adult departments should be asked to accept a certain quota which has been worked out by the finance committee, the pastor, the general superintendent, and the department superintendents in advance.

The teachers and class officers should be consulted and if they desire, the quota of their class may be changed to meet their approval. Class quotas probably will not be assigned in the Intermediate and younger age groups. Again it should be emphasized that the suggested quotas are not assessments. It is hoped that the quotas will be accepted by the classes as goals which they will strive to reach.

In nondepartment Sunday schools, instead of working through department superintendents, the budget committee will work through the teachers and submit to them at the officers and teachers' meeting a suggested quota for each class.

4. *Securing Subscriptions*

The day has arrived for securing the pledges. Department and class quotas should be shown on a blackboard in each department room. A brief explanation should be given by the department superintendent. The teachers should then take charge of their classes. As soon as the reports of the day are made up, the class quota should be explained, the subscription cards passed and every member present urged to make a weekly subscription to the budget fund.

In the Junior and Intermediate departments the matter should be approached with great tact. If the pupils have had it explained before hand they will know how much they should give. Teachers should check with the parents regarding subscriptions made by Juniors or younger children. All teachers and officers who did not sign a card at the workers' meeting should sign now.

In the morning preaching hour, the deacons and finance committee should pass a subscription card to every one present who has not already filled one in, and sufficient time should be allowed to secure his subscription. The pastor should have this matter in hand and see that no one is omitted.

5. *Going Afield for Subscriptions*

In the afternoon the deacons, finance committee, and Sunday school officers and teachers should visit in the homes of all church members and Sunday school pupils who have not been reached. It will be well for a lunch to be served at the church building for all the workers in order that they may get out into the field and into the homes of the people by one o'clock.

Teachers of Young People and Adults will visit and present the matter to members of their classes who were absent from Sunday school.

Workers with Intermediates and younger age groups will visit the parents of their pupils and enlist their co-operation in leading the pupils to have a share in Scriptural giving.

The names of church members not in the Sunday school will have been divided into convenient groups, and placed in the hands of the deacons, finance committee, and others secured to assist in the campaign, who will visit each one and ask him to subscribe to the budget.

The church building should be open all the afternoon and one or more workers should be on hand to receive the subscriptions from any who were not present in the morning services and who prefer to come to the church in the afternoon to make their subscription rather than to be visited in their homes by the committee.

Further opportunity will be given in the Training Union and the evening preaching service for any who have not already done so to fill in subscription cards.

Let the subscription committee and Sunday school officers and teachers press the matter of securing subscriptions each day during the following week. Naturally some will be missed on Sunday. They should be visited in the evening hours during the week and every one given an opportunity to make a subscription to the budget. If this method is pursued with energy and vigor, in a week's time practically the entire Sunday school and church membership can be enlisted to support the budget. The matter should be lovingly and tactfully pressed until a subscription card is signed by every church member and every member of the Sunday school.

6. *Operating the Plan*

It is not enough to set out properly a correct system of church financing and secure subscriptions to the budget. The system must be correctly operated if it is to prove successful. This requires intelligent, painstaking, and never ceasing vigilance and energy.

(1) *A good system of bookkeeping essential*

Make use of the Sunday school records. The plan for using the Sunday school as a church financing agency cannot succeed apart from the correct operation of the Six Point Record System. This system must be installed as planned and operated as per instructions. Let there be no speculating or guess work about it. Follow instructions to the letter and success is assured.

This means that great care is needed to select the right individuals for general secretary, associates, and department and class secretaries. Not only must these workers have skill in record keeping, they must also merit the confidence of the membership in their tact and discretion.

(2) *The church treasurer's records*

The church treasurer's records must be adapted to a Unified Budget. An account should be kept for every individual who contributes to the support of the church's program, children as well as adults, and small givers as well as large givers. Many churches will have to change their system of keeping their treasurer's records. Some large churches may need to employ a church bookkeeper for this particular purpose. All should study ways to improve their system of keeping their records.

(3) *Monthly reports sent*

Each month a card is issued to each pupil in the Sunday school showing his standing on the Six Point Record System and his financial standing on the budget. In making out the monthly Sunday school reports, the Sunday school secretary should secure from the church bookkeeper the financial standing of each member of the Sunday school and should see that it is inserted on his monthly Six Point Record System report, Form 145. These reports are handed to all the pupils present on the first Sunday morning of the month and delivered to all the absentees by teachers or class officers during the following week.

At regular intervals the church treasurer should mail a statement to every church member not in Sunday school showing his pledge and amount subscribed on the budget.

7. *Enlisting New Members*

When a new member joins the Sunday school the teacher should acquaint him with the operation of the financial system of the church. He should be given a letter which has been prepared by the finance committee, a subscription card, and a few of the Six Point Record System weekly report envelopes. The new pupil should not be unduly urged to make a subscription immediately on joining the Sunday school. However, if he does not sign up in a worthy way in a reasonable time the teacher or a class officer should make a personal visit and go into the whole matter with him and secure his subscription.

When a new member joins the church an envelope should be given to him containing a letter explaining the church's financial system, a leaflet on stewardship, a message from the pastor, a subscription card and a few offering envelopes. In the event he does not sign the subscription card in a reasonable time, a visit should be made by one of the members of the finance committee and his subscription secured.

8. *Dealing with Individuals*

It will be necessary for the original finance committee to keep in close touch with the church record and not allow subscribers to the budget to get in arrears for large amounts or for a great length of time. Prompt payers to the budget are needed. When members get in arrears for large amounts, or for a long time, it often has a bad effect upon them. They cease to attend the services regularly and lose interest in the work. Regular giving is a necessary part of spiritual growth.

Sometimes misfortune befalls people; ill health or loss of position renders them unable to meet their financial obligations to their church. These cases should be understood, and subscribers should be relieved of their financial obligations until a new source of revenue is realized. A wise finance committee can render valuable spiritual service at this point.

V. A WORD OF CAUTION

Pastors, Sunday school superintendents, department superintendents, and teachers should not under any circumstances allow the finance committee to exploit the Sunday school as a money gathering agency. They should see that nothing, no matter how important in itself, should in any wise come in to interfere with the Sunday school as a Bible teaching agency.

If the proper wisdom and care are exercised, the Sunday school organization may be used in a wonderful way by the church in the operation of its financial system and in many other useful ways. However, under no circumstances should the leaders ever forget that the main business of the Sunday school is to teach the Word of God. All other things must be rightly related to that main objective.

Use Section VIII of the workbook in the appendix for reviewing this chapter after the class discussion.

CHAPTER IX

THE SUNDAY SCHOOL FUNCTIONING AS A CHURCH MISSIONARY AGENCY

In Acts 1: 8 (ASV) we have recorded the last words of Jesus before his ascension, as follows: "Ye shall be my witnesses both in Jerusalem, and in all Judea and in Samaria, and unto the uttermost part of the earth." It seems logical to compare our local church field to "Jerusalem"; our state mission field to "Judea"; our home mission fields to "Samaria" and our foreign mission fields to the nations designated in the Commission as "the uttermost part of the earth." Our obligation as Christ's witnesses is to give the gospel message to all people everywhere, "beginning at Jerusalem."

It is the purpose in this study to approach this question in as practical a manner as possible. We desire to help our people to realize how our Sunday schools may be utilized by our churches to make the greatest possible contribution toward the education and enlistment of all our people, from the youngest to the oldest, in worldwide missions. We desire to show how our Sunday schools in their plans and operations are linked up with the world program of Southern Baptists.

I. THE FIELD IS THE WORLD

For convenience certain divisional lines have been adopted by Southern Baptists in the arrangement of our missionary work. We will first discuss the fields and then the means we employ in getting our missionary messages to our people. It is our aim to acquaint them with our program for winning the world to Christ, and to enlist every member in every Baptist church to co-operate in this program.

1. *The Local Field*

The territory immediately surrounding each church house is designated as the local field. While no visible lines can be drawn circumscribing any church's territory, at the same time, in cities where there are two or more churches, it is generally understood that each church should observe logical boundaries marked by certain streets or avenues. Of course, this plan cannot apply in all cases and no hard and fast rule can be made in this connection.

For example, some large "down-town" churches must necessarily look far beyond their own immediate locality for a large part of their prospective members. Likewise, in some country communities, one church may cover a territory with a radius of ten miles or more while another rural church would cover a territory perhaps only half so large. The matter of accessibility and the nearness of other Baptist churches would be the deciding factors. Through its branch Sunday schools each church should seek to reach out in all directions at least half-way to the next Baptist church.

It is not enough for churches to build commodious, modern houses of worship, provide attractive preachers, offer good programs of worship, maintain great Sunday schools, Baptist Training Unions, Woman's Missionary Unions, and Baptist Brotherhoods. All these are greatly to be desired, yet many churches have these and still there are multitudes of lost people living under the very shadow of their buildings, few of whom ever attend any of the services. Something more is needed.

Through its Sunday school organization, every church should take a religious census at least once a year, and in this way definitely locate every man, woman, and child in the community who is a stranger to grace. Through its Sunday school organization, every church can and should visit, not only once but as many times as is necessary, every lost person thus located, with an earnest invitation and a loving urge to join the Sunday school and attend the services of public worship. Through the Sunday school organization an energetic, ardent, soul-winning pastor should reach every one of these lost people with an earnest invitation to accept Christ as a personal Saviour.

The local church field is a very definite and important part of the world. It is the beginning point in every church's missionary operation. In his last words to his disciples, Jesus told them to begin at Jerusalem. Any church which so desires may utilize its Sunday school organization in carrying out the commission to reach the last lost man, woman, and child in its local territory.

2. *State Missions*

For the sake of convenience and to simplify and make effective our work, we characterize the next step in our missionary work as state missions. Every state in the territory of the Southern Baptist Convention has an organization with headquarters for the purpose of carrying on missionary work in that particular state.

The work which we call State Missions is usually divided into departments about as follows: Sunday School, Baptist Training Union, Baptist Brotherhood, Baptist Foundation, Baptist Student Union, Church Music, and Evangelism. Some of the states do not divide their work exactly as indicated; some have fewer departments, and others have additional departments according to their needs. Most states maintain a Baptist state paper. All support missionary pastors.

The support of missionary pastors is usually the main channel for missionary work by the different state mission boards. This phase of the work calls for supplementing the salaries of pastors of weak churches, and assisting in the support of pastors in strategic places, in struggling country churches, in industrial centers, and in suburban churches of our great cities.

Following closely the ministry through mission pastors and evangelism comes educational work, which includes Sunday school, Baptist Training Union Woman's Missionary Union, Baptist Brotherhood, and Student Union work.

3. *Home Missions*

The time is not yet in Southern Baptist life when we are agreed that each state can take care of all the missionary work needed to be done within its borders. Some of the states need help from other states because of particular problems.

For example, New Mexico, with a small Baptist constituency and a large Indian and Mexican population, has problems, which do not confront many of the other states. Maryland, with its immigration problems; Texas, with its large Mexican population; Florida, with its large Cuban population; Louisiana, with its thousands of French-speaking people; South Carolina, with its rapidly growing industrial situation; and California, Washington, and Oregon with the challenge of pioneer work; all have their specific needs.

These are exceptional situations, and these states need the co-operation of all the Southern Baptist Convention in taking care of their problems. The Home Mission Board with its headquarters at Atlanta, Georgia, is entrusted with these weighty matters, as well as other types of missionary work now being done by Southern Baptists.

The particular phases of work done by the Home Mission Board include the following:

Evangelism
Work among various language groups
Schools and Good-Will Centers
Work among the Indians
Work among the Negroes
Work among the Deaf Mutes
Cuba, Canal Zone, Panama and Alaska
Southern Baptist chaplains
Work among Migrants
Church Extension
Publicity and Missionary Education
Rescue Missions
Work among the Jews

Through its Department of Co-operative Missions the Home Mission Board works with various state mission boards in maintaining a City Mission Program, a Rural Church Program, a Western Mission Program and a Mountain Mission Program. All of this is missionary work, the ultimate end being to win the lost to Christ as Saviour and Lord.

4. Foreign Missions

While we as Southern Baptists have not yet included in our foreign mission program all the nations of the earth, we have been steadily expanding our Foreign

Mission enterprise. We are supporting missionaries in many countries and territories as follows (except for disruption caused by war and internal conditions): Spain, Italy, Switzerland, Yugoslavia, Hungary, Romania, Nigeria, Gold Coast, Lebanon, Israel, Arabia, Hadhramant, Yemen, Mexico, Guatemala, Honduras, Costa Rica, Brazil, Colombia, Chile, Argentina, Uruguay, Paraguay, China, Japan, Formosa, the Philippines, Hawaii. Our Northern Baptist brethren are maintaining missionaries in many foreign countries not occupied by Southern Baptists.

Southern Baptists carry on the work of Foreign Missions by preaching, teaching, healing (hospital work), and the distribution of literature, Bibles, pages from the Scriptures, papers and tracts. On some of our foreign fields we maintain primary schools, colleges, and seminaries.

We also have publishing houses in which Sunday school literature, books, denominational papers, Baptist Training Union literature, and other materials are printed in the native languages. All of these are proving to be effective agencies through which to reach lost people for Christ and to strengthen and develop an intelligent and virile church membership and splendid native ministry.

Certainly, it should be our earnest prayer and determinate purpose to conduct our missionary affairs as Southern Baptists in such a way as to continue to expand our missionary enterprises and to undergird all our forces in any emergency. All this will result in sustained forward movement in giving the gospel to the waiting nations beyond the seas.

The Sunday school is responsible for promoting the work of these mission boards and of the other boards, institutions, and commissions of the Southern Baptist

Convention, as listed in the annual Calendar of Denominational Activities.

II. How Sunday Schools May Acquaint People with Our Mission Program

Many agencies among Southern Baptists are doing nobly in the way of teaching missions in our churches. Among these are our Woman's Missionary Unions, with their inspiring programs and graded mission study classes; our Baptist Training Unions with their monthly missionary meetings and study courses; and our Brotherhood organizations.

Our Sunday schools are intelligently and earnestly working with a view to provide missionary instruction for the entire Sunday school membership in every Baptist church, acquainting them with our Southern Baptist world program and enlisting them to give of their means for carrying out this program. Let us see how this is being done.

1. *Through Our Sunday School Lessons and Other Literature*

Missionary teaching is an integral part of any Bible-centered lesson material. Every portion of the Bible teaches missions and our periodicals give special emphasis to the subject in the treatment of the lessons.

Both the Graded and Uniform Lesson Series provide abundant missionary materials, presenting the need of all people for the Lord Jesus Christ. Both series of lessons seek to teach the Great Commission and to provide frequent opportunities for boys and girls to have experiences in sharing the gospel with others.

Even Nursery materials teach that "We . . . are helpers" and that one of the best ways to help is by sharing stories of Jesus.   Through song and story the children learn that Jesus loves "all the children of the world."

In the Beginner lessons much emphasis is given to sharing, which includes sharing stories of Jesus and missionary projects for friends at home and far away. Always at least one labeled missionary lesson is included in the course and usually an entire unit seeks to provide for four-and five-year-olds real experiences in telling others about Jesus. By building a concept of Jesus as the best Friend of every child, missions is taught, even to small children.

In the Primary department the indirect teaching of missions continues along with a direct emphasis. Both Graded and Uniform Lessons include stories of boys and girls in other lands, actual missionary events, pictures, and songs. Missionary material is plentiful in both pupils' and teachers' books and the lesson courses include definite missionary units. Missionary Bible verses and programs are used frequently.   In the Junior department missions occupies a major place, in both programs and lesson courses. Both Graded and Uniform Lessons seek to develop the likenesses of all people and the need of all people for the Saviour. Special missionary days are observed and special missionary Bible passages are memorized. True stories from mission fields are included in the pupil's quarterly. The teacher's books contain missionary units, special missionary lessons, missionary pictures, songs, programs, and projects.

Missions is certainly a major emphasis in the programs and lesson materials for Intermediates. In the Closely Graded Series all four units for the spring quarter feature the outreach of the gospel, with special emphasis on our mission responsibilities today.   In addition, there is at least one lesson in the other quarters having a strong missions teaching. The appeal is made with fifteen- and sixteen-year-olds to consider Christian missions as their lifework.

In every Uniform cycle lessons based on the study of Acts, certain epistles, and portions of the Gospels provide needed missions emphases.

Inasmuch as Young People and Adults use Uniform Lessons, the above statement applies to them also.   In addition, missionary teachings for family use are included in the family altar section of *Home Life*.

The Uniform Lesson materials offered for Young People and Adults include a rich fund of information on how Southern Baptists are carrying out the Great Commission through their missionary program.   The lesson treatments have as a major objective the enlistment of every Christian in the whole program, by means of gifts and personal missionary activities.   In addition, missionary teachings for family use are included in the family altar section of *Home Life*.

2. *Through Following the Calendar of Denominational Activities*

One way to make sure that Baptists know more about denominational affairs is for the school to adopt the "Calendar of Denominational Activities," by means of which occasion will be provided for stressing these causes in turn, so that none will be overlooked.

The Calendar of Activities prepared by the Sunday School Department of the Baptist Sunday School Board is based on the items in the denominational calendar. There is variation from year to year, but certain items are basic, such as: State Mission Day in October, Home and Foreign Mission Day in March, Christian Home Week in May, Christian Education, Stewardship, Denominational Papers, and other activities of the denomination at specified times. Copies of the Calendar may be secured from your state Sunday school secretary, or from the Baptist Sunday School Board.

Sunday schools which follow this calendar will provide their members with a curriculum of missionary education designed to keep them informed about all of the work of the denomination.

The plan for educational presentation of these causes is simple and practical. Brief, attractive program material is offered by the Home and Foreign Mission Boards and by the State Mission Boards. Programs may also be found in *The Sunday School Builder,* a monthly publication of the Sunday School Board prepared for all Sunday school officers, teachers, and class officers. From month to month in accord with the Calendar suggested, program material dealing with the denominational causes will appear in the *Builder.*

In class Sunday schools pastor and superintendent may appoint competent individuals to take this material and prepare opening or closing programs for the school as a whole. In a school organized by departments, each superintendent is responsible for the mission programs in his department. The teaching of the lesson will not be interfered with, but the usual time allotted for the assembly will be devoted to an effective presentation, in vivid and instructive fashion, of a brief program on missions, education, or benevolence. Such a program should utilize any missionary applications inherent in the regular Bible lessons of the day. Surely life and enthusiasm would be added to the assembly through this process, and these missionary programs will be a welcome feature to officers, teachers, and pupils alike.

3. *Through Missionary Teaching Inherent in Operating the Unified Budget*

It is believed that a close study of chapter 8, "The Sunday School Functioning as a Church Financing Agency," will convince one that the suggested method of church financing will produce a church membership fully informed and sympathetic with a worldwide missionary program.

It is readily seen that this method commits every Sunday school pupil and every church member to a worldwide missionary program. Of course, each one puts himself and his money into this program voluntarily. However, experience in operating this system of church finance has shown that practically all the people welcome the opportunity to include worldwide missions in their offerings. They are glad to have a part in the spread of the gospel to the ends of the earth.

Annually the publicity campaign in preparation for raising the budget affords an unmatched opportunity to acquaint the people with the matter of stewardship and missions and the obligation of each to participate in a worthy way in the budget. Then, again, making an offering knowing that a part of it each week goes to spread the gospel throughout the ends of the earth keeps the subject of missions ever before each member in a very personal way.

To our way of thinking there has never been devised any method of mission study comparable to this, and eventually it will produce an informed church membership co-operating along all lines of missionary endeavor at home and abroad.

4. *Through the Missionary Section in the Church Library*

Every Baptist church today recognizes the need for church libraries. In every one of these libraries there should be a mission section with books adapted to the needs of all the workers and pupils in the Sunday school. Experience and observation teaches us that books on missions are among the most popular. They are read with great pleasure and profit by children, young people, and adults, alike.

Pastors, officers, and teachers should realize what a wonderful opportunity is afforded through the church library for disseminating missionary information throughout the entire Sunday school membership.

5. *Through the Use of Posters and Pictures*

Some statistician has said that we remember one-eighth of all we hear, five-eighths of all we see, and seven-eighths of all we do. What a combination all these three might be in the teaching of missions in the Sunday school! Posters and pictures mean something to see, giving a visualization that makes real. Further, they furnish that all-important doing for the group responsible for the making of them.

There is a missionary message in every Sunday school lesson, and posters made by the class become a project in expressing the lesson learned. The search for material is of manifold advantage to the pupil, leading him to become interested in the great mission causes and to come to feel a vital part of the wide kingdom work.

One project interesting to young and old is the preparation of a series of posters of the missionaries from his own state, and the work they are doing.

Pastors, educational directors, general superintendents, department superintendents, and teachers need to get a new appreciation of the wonderful opportunity offered in this fertile Sunday school field to study the great subjection of missions. They need to acquaint themselves fully with the scope of Southern Baptist missionary endeavor both as to the magnitude of the task and the practical provisions made for the accomplishment of this task. And with new zeal and determination they need to link up with Christ all their resources for the purpose of making his saving grace known to all men.

Section IX of the workbook in the appendix will help the class members to fix in mind some main points of this chapter.

WORKBOOK

For Review and Application

The activities suggested on these worksheets will serve for review, summary, and application. It is suggested that after the study of each chapter, the class turn to the proper section and follow the instructions given. After all have completed the review, the teacher should lead them in marking their answers (see pp. 152-153). This should be followed by further discussion to clear up any misconceptions, and to apply the conclusions to the local situation as indicated in the instructions on each worksheet.

This material is designed so that class members may work from their books and record answers on a separate sheet to be handed in. (If facilities are available, it will be well to mimeograph each section of the workbook on a separate sheet. If this is done, the class members may answer by checking or filling in the blanks on the mimeographed sheet, instead of a separate paper.)

While these pages are planned for use at the close of each class period as a guide to summarizing and applying the principles discussed, they may also be used as the examination for class members who will need to take a written test (see instructions on p. 7).

SECTION I

1. On a mimeographed sheet, check the statements in the following list which set forth conceptions of the Sunday school which are wrong, or too limited.

If you are working from your book, write your answers on a separate sheet. You need not copy the statements. Copy only the letters which are before those statements that do not give the right conception of the Sunday school.

  a. _____ A self-governing body
  b. _____ An auxiliary of the church
  c. _____ A church agency for carrying out the Great Commission
  d. _____ A unit in a worldwide system
  e. _____ A church agency for teaching children
  f. _____ A once-a-week teaching session

2. Check the letters before the four correct endings to this sentence. A Sunday school is correctly positionized when__

  a. _____ The church elects the officers and teachers
  b. _____ The superintendent reports regularly to the church business meeting
  c. _____ The church finances the Sunday school
  d. _____ The Sunday school treasury is separate from the church treasury
  e. _____ Classes elect their own teachers
  f. _____ The church is responsible for the activities of the Sunday school
  g. _____ Classes and departments raise money for their own activities
  h. _____ Sunday school work is not considered church business

3. If the following sentence is only partly correct, copy from it the things which are the true functions of the Sunday school; if the entire sentence is correct, write OK on your paper:

It is the true function of a Sunday school to teach the Bible, provide employment for church members, reach people, train workers, promote preaching attendance, win to Christ, train in scriptural giving, enlist in missions, and promote the Baptist spirit.

Make a written list of those functions named in the preceding sentence which need more emphasis in your Sunday school (or underline them on your mimeographed sheet). As you study the rest of this book, will you search for ways to strengthen your school in these matters?

SECTION II

Do you believe that your Sunday school could improve its Bible-teaching ministry if it made more effective use of the weekly officers and teachers' meeting? If so, will you find in this list the things which you believe should be done in your weekly meetings? On a separate sheet, copy the numbers to indicate which things you selected (or check them on your mimeographed sheet). After you have finished your list, select the three or four items you believe need most immediate emphasis in your school, and encircle the numbers which indicate these items.

Our school will improve its Bible-teaching ministry if we will use our weekly officers and teachers' meetings to—

1. _____ See that classes keep on trying to reach members who are habitually absent.
2. _____ Make visitation assignments to classes, receive reports from teachers of visiting done by classes, and pray for needs discovered by visitors.
3. _____ Lead all officers and teachers to understand the need for more classes and closer grading by ages.

4. _____ Study records and plan ways to get each class member to do the six things included in the record system.

5. _____ Plan assembly programs to use the talents of our members.

6. _____ Lead teachers to plan for Bible using and class participation in the lesson discussions.

7. _____ Help teachers plan ways to get members to study the lesson.

8. _____ Guide officers and teachers to do more effective Bible study.

9. _____ Encourage workers to regular, personal study of books and literature on Sunday school work.

10. _____ Pray specifically about our needs and problems.

Since your school cannot achieve these things without a good weekly officers and teachers' meeting, will you be one who will co-operate to maintain such a meeting? Write *yes* or *no* on your paper.

SECTION III

A. Copy the numbers of these statements on a separate sheet (unless you are working on a mimeographed paper). Put a cross by the numbers of the wrong statements. In the discussion after the test be ready to tell why you disagree.

1. In a Sunday school only the experienced Christians should be used in service.

2. A functioning Sunday school should furnish a place of service for every church member.

3. One weakness of the modern Sunday school is that it calls for so many officers and teachers.

4. One strong point of the modern Sunday school is that it puts many Christians to work.
5. Assembly programs should use the talent of the members.
6. It is well to depend on outside talent to put on special features in assembly programs.

B. Copy the figures to indicate talents which your Sunday school can use, (or check on mimeographed sheet.) When the class discusses the answers, be ready to tell how you would use the individuals with these talents.

1. _____ Play a stringed instrument
2. _____ Lead games
3. _____ Keep accurate records
4. _____ Lead other people to do things
5. _____ Know and love books
6. _____ Lead singing
7. _____ Visit tactfully
8. _____ Plan assembly programs
9. _____ Cheer up a shut-in
10. _____ Make posters
11. _____ Drive a car
12. _____ Arrange flowers

Will you make a list of unused talents in your class or department, and give it to your superintendent with suggestions about ways in which these talents may be used in assemblies, in Sunday school administration or teaching, and in class activities? This may be done at home.

SECTION IV

From this list select all the things which you believe your Sunday school ought to do in order to reach more people. On a separate sheet copy the numbers to indicate your selections (or encircle the numbers on your mimeographed sheet). Put a check by the number of each point you are willing to help put into effect.

1. Accept responsibility for the territory halfway to the nearest Baptist church in every direction.

2. Determine places in this complete territory where branch Sunday schools are needed. (Can you write the names of places where such schools are needed?)

3. Take a census of all your territory.

4. Make it a practice to take a census annually, or more often.

5. Provide enough workers for the new units your school will need in order to reach all your responsibilities. (Name some new units which will be needed.)

6. Set up all your classes on an age basis.

7. Assign all prospects on an age basis to the proper classes.

8. Plan space for the people whom your school ought to reach, without waiting until they begin to attend.

9. Assign each lost person on your rolls and prospect lists to the proper class as its responsibility.

10. Expect each class to follow up the unaffiliated Baptists among its members and prospects.

11. Use the weekly officers and teachers' meeting to make visitation assignments by classes and to receive reports from teachers on the visitation they have led their classes to do.

12. Maintain a regular weekly and monthly schedule for visitation.

13. Seek to enlist every Christian in your classes in visitation.

14. Ask visitors, even when visiting for one class or department, to make reports on all members of the family not enrolled.

15. Visit not only to bring back absentees and win new members, but also to encourage members to build the six habits involved in the record system.

SECTION V

A. On a separate sheet copy the numbers from 1-10. After each number write *True* or *False* for the sentence it indicates. (If you have a mimeographed sheet, mark each sentence *T* or *F*.)

1. If an individual is a success in other fields, he does not need to train for Sunday school work.

2. No Sunday school worker can render his best service unless he is willing to train.

3. The Sunday School Training Course offers books for all people fifteen years of age or older who wish to grow as Christians.

4. The Sunday School Training Course is limited to officers and teachers.

5. If an individual is willing to learn by experience, the study of books is of little value.

6. A Sunday school clinic offers training through both theory and practice.

7. Good weekly officers and teachers' meetings will provide a continuous program of practical, in-service training.

8. The Sunday school and Training Union courses are entirely separate and unrelated.

9. The only accepted plan for a training course is two periods a night for five nights.

10. The source for enough good workers for any Sunday school is the unused church members who need to be enlisted for training.

B. Copy (or check on your mimeographed sheet) all the letters which indicate true endings to this sentence:

In your Sunday school, training for workers, prospective workers, and class members above fifteen years of age can be provided through—

a. Training schools
b. Home study of books in the Sunday School Training Course
c. Weekly officers and teachers' meetings
d. Class Officers' clinics
e. Teachers' guidance in the activities of the class
f. Direct practice in doing Sunday school work

Now put an x by the letters which indicate things you believe your Sunday school is doing well. Draw a circle around each letter that indicates a point which your Sunday school needs to emphasize more.

SECTION VI

On a separate sheet copy the numbers which indicate things your school does, or should do, to improve the attendance at the preaching service, (or encircle the numbers on your mimeographed sheet).

1. Bring into the preaching service practically every person who attends Sunday school.

2. Give special attention to have the lost Sunday school members attending preaching.

3. Have such good teaching that members do not need the preaching service.

4. Tell workers that if they get people to attend preaching that will do instead of personal soul-winning.

5. Use the Unified Service to encourage preaching attendance.

6. In the weekly officers and teachers' meeting, study records on preaching attendance and plan how to improve.

7. In the weekly officers and teachers' meetings plan assembly programs to magnify preaching attendance.

8. Use the weekly officers and teachers' meetings to help teachers develop skill in using lesson materials to teach the value of worship.

9. Hold officers and teachers responsible for the attendance of class members.

10. If you have, or ever should have, only part-time preaching use the Sunday school to provide a service of worship on the Sundays the pastor is not there.

When you discuss your answers in class, decide how your school can improve its efforts to secure preaching attendance. Consider this sentence and decide if you agree: "It is sinful for a church not to use its Sunday school to get lost people into the preaching service." Compare your conclusion with James 4:17.

SECTION VII

A. Number a sheet from 1 to 5. After each number copy the letter or letters to indicate the correct ending to the sentence. (On a mimeographed sheet, the right endings may be checked).

1. If your church were to go for months without winning one soul to Christ, the reason would probably be because—

    a. None of the members desire to see souls saved.
    b. The church lacks a positive program for evangelism.
    c. The church is without a pastor.

2. An adequate program of evangelism for your church would need to have several of the following characteristics, namely—

    a. All church members enlisted in soul-winning
    b. Outside evangelists always utilized
    c. Continuous, systematic, planned program
    d. A church program
    e. Led by pastor working through Sunday school
    f. Depending on Decision Days in the Sunday school
    g. Every class and department of the Sunday school participating in soul-winning

3. Two of the most important elements for an effective soul-winning program in your church are:

    a. Advertising
    b. Planning
    c. Money
    d. Prayer
    e. Special music
    f. A comfortable building

4. The best opportunity to develop your Sunday school workers as soul-winners is in a planned program of visitation promoted through—

    a. Monthly workers' council
    b. Weekly officers and teachers' meeting
    c. Letters from the church office

5. If there are no lost people on its class roll, an adult class should be—

    a. Praised

    b. Criticised

    c. Stimulated to visit to enrol new members

B. Answer these questions according to your sincere conviction about the situation in your church. Number from 1 to 5 and answer with *yes* or *no*. You may qualify your answer if you wish.

1. Does your church win souls continuously, all the year round?

2. You selected five characteristics of an adequate evangelistic program as you completed the second sentence in the foregoing part of this test. Does the evangelistic program in your church have these five characteristics?

3. Do most of your members believe that the pastor's main ministry is to lead them to be soul-winners?

4. In the weekly officers and teachers' meeting is there regular prayer and planning for soul-winning through your Sunday school?

5. Does every class and every department in your Sunday school really major on soul-winning?

When you discuss this test in class, decide how the evangelistic efforts of your church can be improved so that you could answer each of the foregoing questions with an unqualified "yes."

SECTION VIII

Arrange your paper for two columns. Head one "Good Financial Program," and the other "Poor Finances." Put each item in the following list under the proper column. You may do this by writing the numbers of the items without copying the statements.

1. In arrears for running expenses
2. Missions included in the regular budget
3. Spiritual starvation
4. Only large givers enlisted
5. All members included
6. High-powered, special collection
7. A systematic, planned program
8. Small contributors overlooked
9. Under church control
10. Some denominational causes not supported
11. One treasury for all phases of church life
12. In arrears for missions
13. Based on prayerfully prepared budget
14. Nonchurch members overlooked
15. Each organization with a separate treasury
16. Operated through the Sunday school
17. Spasmodic efforts
18. Included in the Six Point Record System
19. All church members kept informed of the church record of their gifts
20. Regular income meets current expenses

Now pick out from the foregoing list the items which describe the financial program of your church, and circle the numbers on your paper which indicate the items you select. Are they all in the "good" column? Is your church engaging in any practices which must be listed as "poor"? When you discuss this test in class, decide what changes, if any, you would like to see made in the financial program of your church. Decide how your Sunday school can be used to help bring about these changes.

SECTION IX

Which of the following things do you believe your school should do, or continue to do, in order to function as a missionary agency? On a separate sheet copy the numbers before the statements which you select. (Encircle on mimeographed sheet.) Put checks by the numbers of those things which you will help put into effect, according to your ability and opportunity.

1. Take a religious census at least once a year.
2. Assign all names of lost people to the proper classes.
3. Visit lost people repeatedly to win them to Christ.
4. Present a program on State Missions each October.
5. Observe Home and Foreign Mission Day in March.
6. Have other special programs presenting the denominational causes as listed in the Sunday School Calendar of Activities.
7. Ask the church to provide mission literature in the library.
8. Use the weekly officers and teachers' meeting to plan lessons with missionary emphasis.
9. Use *The Sunday School Builder* as an aid in following the Calendar of Activities.
10. Operate the Unified Budget in a way to teach missions.

In the class discussion of the answers be ready to indicate particular ways in which you may co-operate in the things which you have agreed to help put into practice (as indicated by the numbers you checked).

ANSWERS AND SCORING INSTRUCTIONS

SECTION I.—1. *a, b, d, e, f;* 2. *a, b, c, f,* (Score one point for each correct answer, less one for each error); 3. OK (Score one point). For sincere, thoughtful selection of greatest needs of your Sunday school, and prayerful willingness to study ways to strengthen the work, each individual should score an additional ten points.

Total score on test *20 points*

SECTION II.—All ten points should be selected. Score one point for each number copied, plus five points for sincere selection of any matters needing emphasis, and for agreement to co-operate.

Total score on test *15 points.*

SECTION III.—1.—Cross by 1, 3, and 6. Score one point for each number correctly marked, less one point for each error. 2. Score one point for each talent checked, if individual has in mind a specific way to use that talent in Sunday school.

Total score on test *15 points.*

SECTION IV.—Score one point for each number selected, and an additional two points for each number checked, if the individual is sincerely willing to co-operate in getting done the things indicated.

Total score on test *45 points.*

SECTION V.—A. Mark *True* 2, 3, 6, 7, 10. Mark *False* 1, 4, 5, 8, 9. Score one for each sentence correctly marked, less one for each error. B. All letters should be copied or checked. For sincere following of all instructions given, allow ten points.

Total score on test *20 points.*

SECTION VI.—A. Correct sentences are 1, 2, 5, 6, 7, 8, 9, 10. Score one point for each correct answer, less one for each error.

Total score on test *10 points.*

SECTION VII.—A. 1-*b;* 2-*a, c, d, e, g;* 3-*b, d;* 4-*b;* 5-*c.* (Score one point for each correct answer. Subtract one point for each wrong answer.)   B. Score one point for each question sincerely answered.

Total score on test *15 points.*

SECTION VIII.—A. Under "Good Financial Program" list 2, 5, 7, 9, 11, 13, 16, 18, 19, 20. List other items under "Poor Finances." Score one point for each item placed in correct column. Subtract one point for each item listed in the wrong column.   B. Allow ten additional points for sincere evaluation of the local program.

Total score on test *30 points.*

SECTION IX.—Score one point for each item selected as something your school should do, and two additional points for each item checked.

Total score on test *30 points.*

NOTE: Individual using the workbook as a test for home study should have a total score of at least 130 points to grade 70% or over. If a student misses some of the class periods, the teacher may ask him to use designated workbook sections for the required test. However, he must meet the required attendance (see p. 7) to be eligible for the class test for credit.